SPANISH

Beginner's Step-by-Step Course to Quickly Learning the Spanish Language, Spanish Grammar & Spanish Phrases

© Copyright 2016 – All rights reserved.

In no way is it legal to reproduce, duplicate, or transmit any part of this document in either electronic means or in printed format. Recording of this publication is strictly prohibited and any storage of this document is not allowed unless with written permission from the publisher. All rights reserved.

The information provided herein is stated to be truthful and consistent, in that any liability, in terms of inattention or otherwise, by any usage or abuse of any policies, processes, or directions contained within is the solitary and utter responsibility of the recipient reader. Under no circumstances will any legal responsibility or blame be held against the publisher for any reparation, damages, or monetary loss due to the information herein, either directly or indirectly.

Respective authors own all copyrights not held by the publisher.

Legal Notice:

This e-book is copyright protected. This is only for personal use. You cannot amend, distribute, sell, use, quote or paraphrase any part or the content within this e-book without the consent of the author or copyright owner. Legal action will be pursued if this is breached.

Disclaimer:

Please note the information contained within this document is for educational and entertainment purposes only. Every attempt has been made to provide accurate, up to date and reliable complete information. No warranties of any kind are expressed or implied. Readers acknowledge that the author is not engaging in the rendering of legal, financial, medical or professional advice.

By reading this document, the reader agrees that under no circumstances are we responsible for any losses, direct or indirect, which are incurred as a result of the use of information contained within this document, including, but not limited to, errors, omissions, or inaccuracies.

About this Book

This book is divided into 20 chapters, each of which helps teach you how to start speaking Spanish immediately. The book begins by laying down some ground rules for learning how to speak Spanish. The next section talks about the Spanish alphabet and how to pronounce the letters thereof. You're then given some quick differences between Spanish and English that you should be aware of as you start the learning process. The subsequent chapters show you how to speak Spanish in different situations. The second-to-last chapter describes some common mistakes you are likely to make when learning Spanish as a beginner and how to avoid them. The final chapter gives you some short stories to help build your conversational Spanish skills, which are highly important in learning a new language.

All of these chapters combined provide you with a basis and guide to begin your Spanish speaking endeavor with confidence. The tools and exercises in this book will give you the ability to start using Spanish in your everyday life almost immediately, as well as the confidence to do so without worrying you'll make a fool of yourself. This book will be your teacher and your reference guide in the future should you need to refresh your memory or brush up on your skills. This short book is by no means as comprehensive as a college degree in Spanish, but it does provide an in-depth study of the Spanish language and the process of learning a new language in general. It will allow you to begin communicating with native Spanish speakers and start adding Spanish to your everyday life.

Please see the following Table of Contents for more detailed information on how the book is structured.

TABLE OF CONTENTS

Introduction 15

Chapter One The Basics 19

   How to learn a new language 19

   Important tips for learning Spanish (or any other language) . 19

      Set your goal 19

      Practice... 20

      Enhancing your accent 21

      Make friends 22

      Don't get frustrated 22

      Learn more 23

      Make Spanish labels 23

      Think in Spanish 23

      Use circumlocution and contextualization 24

Chapter Two Pronunciation 27

   Vowels 27

   Diphthongs 28

   Consonants 30

Chapter Three Basic Spanish Grammar 35

   Gender 35

   Adjective and noun agreement 36

   Verb changes 37

   Personal pronouns 38

   Singular and plural 38

Capitalization *40*

Chapter Four Basic General Words and Phrases 41

Greetings *41*

Courtesy *42*

Holidays and special occasions *43*

Introducing yourself *43*

Simple questions *44*

Responses and common questions *44*

Simple emergency words *46*

Chapter Five Numbers 49

1 – 20 .... *49*

21 – 100 .... *50*

100 – 1,000 .... *53*

Telling the time *54*

Days of the week *55*

Months *56*

Seasons *57*

Weather *57*

Colors *62*

Animals *64*

Chapter Six Family and Friends 75

Vocabulary *75*

Phrases 78

Meeting new people 79

Nationality 81

    Phrases 83

Chapter Seven Moving Around 85

   At the Airport 85

    Vocabulary 85

    Phrases 87

   Asking for directions 90

   Means of transport 92

   Places 92

    Vocabulary 92

    Phrases 94

   At the Beach 98

    Vocabulary 98

    Phrases 99

Chapter Eight Food, Cooking and Restaurants 103

   Fruits 103

   Vegetables 105

   Meats 106

   Dairy 107

   Drinks 108

   Phrases & cooking instructions 108

 At a restaurant *110*
  Basic restaurant concepts 110
  Table objects 111
  Ordering 112

Chapter Nine Hobbies 119
 Conversations about hobbies *120*

Chapter Ten Emergencies 123
 Emergency services *123*
  Vocabulary 123
  Phrases 124

 Medical help *127*
  Vocabulary 127
  Phrases 136

 Toiletries *139*
  Vocabulary 139
  Phrases 140

Chapter Eleven At the Hotel 143
 Vocabulary *143*

 Phrases *145*

Chapter Twelve Shopping 151
 Vocabulary *151*

 Phrases *154*

Chapter Thirteen Post Office and Movies 159
 Post office *159*
  Vocabulary 160

    Phrases 160
   Movie Theater *162*
    Vocabulary 162
    Phrases 164

Chapter Fourteen Feelings and Emotions 167
   Vocabulary *167*
   Phrases *169*

Chapter Fifteen Love and Relationships 171
   Vocabulary *171*
   Phrases *172*
   At a wedding *174*
    Vocabulary 175
    Phrases 176

Chapter Sixteen Jobs 179
   Vocabulary *179*
    Professions 179
    Applying for a job 180
   Phrases *181*

Chapter Seventeen Sports 185
   Vocabulary *185*
   Phrases *194*

Chapter Eighteen House and Furniture 197

Chapter Nineteen Common Mistakes Made As People Learn

Spanish 207
   False Friends 208
   Sentence Order 209
   Gender of Words... 209
   Date 210
   Misuse of the Word "American" 210

Chapter Twenty Short Stories and Questions 211
   Short Story Number One 212
      Spanish 212
      English 213
      English Questions & Answers 214
      Spanish Questions & Answers...................................... 215
      Phrases for Practice 217
   Short Story Number Two 221
      Spanish 221
      English 224
      English Questions & Answers 226
      Spanish Questions & Answers...................................... 228
      Phrases for Practice 229

Conclusion 237

Key Takeaways 239

How to Put This Information into Action 241

Bonus Resources 243

13 | SPANISH

INTRODUCTION

Have you been thinking about learning a new language? Is Spanish one you're considering? Well, Spanish is at the top of the list of the most widely-spoken languages; in fact, over 500 million people are native Spanish speakers, so by that measure it's the second most popular language after Mandarin Chinese. Besides, research has proven that it is the most romantic language! Whether you want to learn Spanish just to broaden your knowledge or so that you can speak it when you travel to a Spanish-speaking country, you definitely need a guide to make the learning process easier.

If you're not trying to pass a Spanish grammar class, this is the best book for you because it will get you talking the language fast. In any case, you really don't have to be a linguistics professor to speak a language! This book will teach you how to speak Spanish using practical examples and will walk you through conversations to help you get your point across when you're meeting new people, going shopping, going for an interview, going to a restaurant, traveling, asking for directions etc. In simple terms, it will teach you how to speak Spanish in practically any situation.

You won't find boring grammar rules and lessons that you probably wouldn't bother with anyway; instead, you will find practical examples and notes that will help you understand how to actually speak. However, there will be words of warning so you don't end up with egg on your face, so to speak. While Spanish is not as confusing to learn as English – for example, there are not so many homophones (words that sound the same but have different spellings and/or meanings) – the language does have its own little quirks which you need to be aware of.

There are some different reasons for wanting to learn the Spanish language. Being bilingual (knowing two different languages) will make you highly desirable on the job market and will give you a greater sense of self-worth when you can step in and help people struggling with the language barrier out in public. How many times have you seen someone speaking Spanish struggling to communicate with another individual and you standing there, wishing you could help? Now you no longer have to be a bystander, you can step in and take control and help out both individuals. Not only is learning a new language beneficial to your resume and your self-worth, but it's also an excellent way to keep your brain exercising. They say never to stop learning – so learning a new language can be your first step to continuing education.

As you go on with the learning journey, you will also find important tips that will make comprehension and speaking a lot easier. Using this guide, you really can be speaking Spanish in no time at all. *Buen viaje* and the best of luck!

CHAPTER ONE

THE BASICS

How to Learn a New Language

Learning a new language is not as complicated as many people think it is; just remember the things discussed in this chapter and you'll soon increase your fluency. The most difficult step is to get going, so instead of putting it off, start learning right now.

Let's start with some important tips that will help you get a good grasp of the Spanish language.

Important tips for learning Spanish (or any other language)

Set your goal

Setting a daily goal will keep you constantly disciplined while learning a new language. If you have tried learning another language with little or no success, the problem may have been that you didn't have any goal. Set a SMART goal – i.e., it should be Specific, Measurable, Attainable, Realistic, and Time-bound.

If you are wondering how to set SMART goals when learning a language, try this one:

Know what you want to achieve by learning Spanish. You can say that you want to be able to talk in Spanish for five minutes within five weeks of studying the language by learning two pages of Spanish every day and listening to five minutes of audio on how to speak Spanish.

If you practice one day and then again the next week, or twice a week, you'll never reach your goal. It is important to be constant, and by constant, I mean you need to practice every single day. Try to set a goal, for instance, one chapter a day, one page a day, five phrases a day, and so on.

Practice

How will you succeed if you never practice? Learning how to speak a new language is very involved. Think of it like learning how to fly; you can't fly for an hour if you have never flown for five minutes. It is also like learning how to swim; no matter how much video, audio or text on swimming you study, you won't learn if you don't actually get in the water and swim. It's the same with languages.

If it's not practical to speak to someone in Spanish every day, why not team up with a native Spanish speaker on social media who is learning English? Then you can both practice your newly learned skills via email and Skype.

Enhancing your accent

You can watch Spanish movies or a few YouTube videos in order to improve your accent (those with subtitles are a lot easier to follow). You can also listen to music to acquire better pronunciation. Use a dictionary when you don't know a word, practice pronouncing Spanish words by yourself, and keep trying hard until you get it right.

A note about online translators like Google Translator: I am trilingual and I can confidently tell you that online translators cannot teach you how to pronounce words, phrases and sentences correctly. In fact, they will probably mess up your progress in mastering your accent. Although they can help a little, they won't teach you how to actually say things like a native would. So, don't just rush to Google Translator to help you pronounce words. Instead, I would recommend searching for and listening to real people speaking Spanish. YouTube is probably the easiest place to find such people. You can also check out the translations for different songs online (you need the lyrics and audio for both languages so that you can compare as you listen to the songs), or read and listen to a Spanish Bible as you compare to an English Bible (ensure it is the same version).

Make friends

Try as much as possible to make new friends who can speak Spanish and speak to them in Spanish. Don't be embarrassed that your Spanish is not as fluent as theirs to begin with. You can only perfect your Spanish by speaking it. You might even say —I am pregnant‖ when you're trying to say —I am embarrassed‖; it happens, but don't be so cautious that you don't end up speaking much Spanish. In fact, you will probably learn from your mistakes as you interact with people.

Tip: If you are looking for someone to speak Spanish with, head over to one of the freelancing sites like Upwork (formerly oDesk), Freelancer and Elance and hire a native
Spanish speaker. It's free to post a job, and you'll find many Spanish teachers whose rates are quite reasonable.

Don't get frustrated

If you can't get it right, don't get frustrated. Sometimes we have a bad day or we are not in the mood, but no matter why you're not getting it, don't get desperate. If you are practicing and practicing but you can't get it right, it might be because you are tired, so stop and try later. Go for a walk, relax, and then come back to try again, and if you still can't get it, try the next day or ask for someone's help.

Learn more

Even if you are learning through a phrasebook, it might not have enough vocabulary. There is always something new to learn: new words, new phrases, new scenarios, etc. Actively seek out new words you don't know and would like to learn. An easy way to start is to learn about common things that you have at home or at your office. Just write down the words for the various items. Start in your room by writing the names of things you find there, like shoes, then the Spanish words for them (‚shoes' in Spanish is ‚zapatos'), then the pronunciation for each word. After making a list, set a goal to learn five words daily. You can even make flashcards and put a word and its translation on each side. In short, if you see something you could be learning, go ahead and learn it!

Make Spanish labels

Get stickers and label literally everything in your house with the Spanish word and a sentence or two in Spanish. This will expose you to a Spanish environment and help you orient your mind to think in Spanish, because you will be constantly reminded of how to say different things in Spanish.

Think in Spanish

If you are used to thinking in English, this is going to be a tough one, but it is worth the effort. Push yourself to converse with yourself and think in Spanish. Let that inner voice within you talk to you in Spanish. Talk to yourself and do whatever else you usually do subconsciously in English.

Use circumlocution and contextualization

We all find ourselves having a hard time remembering a word, name or phrase even when speaking in English, especially when talking about technical things. I am talking about the times when you find yourself saying ―Yes, that one‖ in the middle of a conversation because you can't remember the right name or phrase for something. Use this to your benefit when learning Spanish or any other language. In this case, you can try to explain things in context. For instance, if you cannot remember how to say ‗a cup' in Spanish, don't fret; you can try to explain it in several other words, like ―the thing that people use to drink tea!‖

Also, try to understand meaning by understanding the context. You really don't need to know the meaning of every single word in Spanish because you can use the contextualization strategy to understand everything that people are talking about.

To summarize, when you set out to learn a new language, you need to immerse yourself in it. It's no good going to a lesson or reading a chapter out of a self-teaching book like this once a week, then forgetting about it until the next week. You need to learn something every day, and practice what you've learned. Come up with creative ways to remember new words and phrases, and you will soon be speaking Spanish without even thinking about it. It's not just what you learn – how you learn is important too!

CHAPTER TWO

PRONUNCIATION

Pronunciation is important in any language, so get the hang of this before attempting to speak to anyone. These days, it's much easier, because there are numerous videos online to help you. In this chapter, you'll learn how to pronounce individual letters by fitting them into common, easily pronounced Spanish words.

One major advantage of Spanish over English is that with most words, the pronunciation is phonetic – the words sound just like they are spelled. There are very few homophones to confuse you. That's words like *there, their, they're* which sound the same but have totally different meanings and spellings. Here's a quick guide to Spanish pronunciation.

VOWELS

In Spanish, there are just five vowels and one sound for each vowel.

- /a/ – ah – The 'a' is pronounced as if you were gargling.

Open your mouth wide and pronounce as *father* and *saw*. Try: mapa, agua.

- /e/ – eh – The ‚e' sound doesn't exactly exist in English; the closest pronunciation might be ‚eh' as *met* and *red*. Don't pronounce the ‚e' as in English! Try: verde, enero.
- /i/ – ee – The ‚i' sound is pretty much like ‚ee' as *feet* and *bee*. The ‚i' sound is very different than the English pronunciation. Try: fino, mi.
- /o/ – oh – The letter ‚o' is pronounced as ‚oh' but with a shorter sound as *boat* and *know*. Try: coco, roto.
- /u/ – oo – It's pronounced as ‚oo' like in *boot* or *do*. Try: futuro, muro.

DIPHTHONGS

A diphthong is a sound formed by the combination of two vowels in a single syllable, in which the sound begins as one vowel and moves toward another.

- ai, ay – /a/+/i/ – The ‚ai' and ‚ay' sound like *why* and *ay*! Try: aire, mayo.
- au – /a/+/u/ – The ‚au' sounds like the expression *auch*! Try: aunque, aula.
- eu – /e/+/u/ – There is not really a sound for this in English; it's something like *ew*, but using the ‚e' sound as *bed* and the ‚u' as *do*. Try: Europa, deudor.

- ei, ey – /e/+/i/ – The pronunciation of 'ei' and 'ey' is close to *hey* and *say*. Try: reina, buey.
- ia – /i/+/a/ – The 'ia' sounds like *yah* and *tiara*. Try: piano, anciano.
- ie – /i/+/e/ – The 'ie' sounds like *yes*. Try: tierra, fiera.
- io – /i/+/o/ – The 'io' is pronounced as *yo-yo* or *John*. Try: radio, río.
- iu – /i/+/u/ – The 'iu' is pronounced as *you*. Try: ciudad, viuda.
- oi, oy – /o/+/i/ – The 'oi' and 'oy' sound like *toy* and *boy*. Try: hoy, heroico.
- ua – /u/+/a/ – The 'ua' is pronounced as *water*. Try: actuar, aduana.
- ue – /u/+/e/ – The 'ue' sounds like *wet*. Try: Huevo, sueño.
- ui – /u/+/i/ – The 'ui' sounds like *we* and *wheat*. Try: arruinar, huir.
- uo – /u/+/o/ – The 'uo' sounds like *quote* and *continuous*. Try: individuo, cuota.

CONSONANTS

A number of Spanish consonants are pronounced differently from their English counterparts. If you can, try to listen to a native speaker and hear how they handle them.

- b – beh – The letter ‚b' is pronounced after l, m or n, and the sound is close to *Venice* and *bear*, although the lips shouldn't touch. Try: bonito.
- c – ceh – The letter ‚c' sounds as *cereal* before e or i. Otherwise it may sound like ‚k' as *computer*. Try: cereza as ‚c', computadora as ‚k'.
- ch – cheh – Try: chocolate, chico.
- d – deh – Try: dust, dos.
- f – effe – The letter ‚f' sounds the same as in the English *Eiffel* or *fountain*. Try: familia.
- g – heh – The ‚g' sounds like *her* before e or i. Otherwise, it sounds like *got* or *get*. Try: gesto as ‚her', guante as ‚get'.
- h – hache – The ‚h' in Spanish is silent. Try: hilo.
- j – hotah – The letter ‚j' sounds like *horse* or *harsh*, never like *jar* or *jump*. Try: jirafa.
- k – kah – The ‚k' sounds the same as in English; it's pronounced as *car* or *key*. Try: koala.
- l – ele – The letter ‚l' is pronounced as *lord* or *like*. Try: lobo.
- ll – doble ele, elle – The double ‚l' is pronounced as the ‚y' in *yesterday*. Try: calle.

- m – emeh – The letter ‗m' is the same as in the English *mother* or *man*. Try: modo.
- n – eneh – The letter ‗n' sounds the same as in the English *no* and *note*. Try: nosotros.
- ñ – enyeh – The ‗ñ' is not another ‗n'; it sounds as *lasagna*, *onion* or *canyon*. Try: niña.
- p – peh – The letter ‗p' sounds the same as in the English *pet* or *paste*. Try: pelo.
- q – koo – The letter ‗q' is pronounced as *curious*. When written with ‗ui' and ‗ue', the ‗u' is silent. For example, ‗¿quién?' is pronounced as /kien/ and ‗¿qué?' as /ke/ (using the Spanish ‗e'). Try: qué, quién.
- r – ere – The ‗r' sounds like *brr* at the beginning of a word; otherwise, it sounds like *break* or *brown*. Try: crear as ‗break', ratón as ‗brr'.
- rr – erre – The double ‗r' sounds like the ‗r' at the beginning of a word. Its sound is more vibrated, as *room* or as the sound of a car accelerating. Try: perro.
- s – ese – The letter ‗s' sounds the same as in the English *sorry* or *sea*. Try: solo.
- sh – Esse/hacheh – The ‗sh' sounds as *shampoo* or *show*. Try: show.

- t – teh – The letter 't' is pronounced as in English, although your tongue has to touch the back of your teeth as in *tea* and *test*. Try: tela.
- v – veh – The letter 'v' is pronounced as the letter 'b', but the lips are touched very mildly as *various* or *voice*. Try: vecino.
- w – doble veh – The letter 'w' has the same pronunciation as in the English *whisky* and *wine*. Try: kiwi.
- x – equis – The letter 'x' is pronounced as 'ks' or 'gs' like in *explosion* or *excited*. Try: xilófono
- y – ye/i griega – The letter 'y' is similar to the double 'l', but with a small difference, as *crayon* and *yellow*. Try: yegua.
- z – setah – The letter 'z' is pronounced as 'th', not as in *zip* or *zero*. Try: zorro.

To make it easier for you to pronounce the letters as the native Spanish speakers do, you can listen to an audio (http://www.languageguide.org/spanish/alphabet/) to ensure that you get it right. Just pass the cursor over each letter of the alphabet to get a feel for how to say it like a native.

DON'T use translation software to learn how to pronounce any word in Spanish or any other language, because these applications don't have the needed accent to make you accurately pronounce words. I have tried it in several languages and I can confidently tell you that such software will screw up your accent learning process.

DO search for real people speaking Spanish on YouTube and other video platforms. These are a lot more likely to be speaking the right Spanish, which simply means that you can learn more and much faster. I know I mentioned this already, but I think it is paramount to reiterate the point.

I have included links to a few YouTube videos to help you in building your pronunciation and accent. You can search for more information on your own (a good student does private study, right?).

To see the glaring pronunciation differences between native Spanish speakers and the translation software, try inputting some of the words you hear the native speakers say to the translation software and see what it comes up with.

It's worth spending some time on getting the pronunciation right, because it will make everything else so much simpler as you learn more and more Spanish. Don't be in such a hurry to learn to speak Spanish that you take short cuts with the pronunciation.

CHAPTER THREE

BASIC SPANISH GRAMMAR

Don't stress out about Spanish grammar. It's nowhere near as complicated as English, and the Spanish people are pretty laid back about it. That said, there are certain points of Spanish grammar you need to be familiar with if you're going to be understood.

GENDER

Spanish has no neutral nouns, in contrast to English, which uses 'the' to refer to someone or something regardless of gender. For example:

English	Masculino (Masculine)	Femenino (Feminine)
Dog	Perro	Perra
Teacher	Maestro	Maestra
Kid	Niño	Niña

In most cases, there is no masculine or feminine gender for a word, meaning that there is no choice and the word already has a gender. It's no big deal if you get the gender wrong – most people will be able to understand your meaning from the context of the sentence. However, there is one notable exception. *El pollo* is a chicken – whether it's running around in the farm yard or cooking in the oven. *La polla* is a slang word for a certain part of male anatomy! For example:

English	Masculino (Masculine)	Femenino (Femenine)
Car	Carro, Coche	----
Book	Libro	----
House	-----	Casa
Lamp	Lámpara	----

Word Order

Spanish seems to have a reversed word order in that an adjective goes after a noun. For instance, instead of saying a black car, you say car black (*coche negro*).

ADJECTIVE AND NOUN AGREEMENT

In Spanish, adjectives agree with the gender (masculine or feminine) and the number (i.e., plural or singular). For instance, we say the black cat (*la gata negra*) or the red cars (*los carros rojos*).

VERB CHANGES

Here's an illustration to help you grasp how verbs change in Spanish. If you did Latin at school and had to conjugate verbs, you'll already have an idea of how it works.

There are five verb changes in Spanish that I will illustrate with the verb 'run': I run (*corro*), you run (*corres*), he or she runs (*corre*), we run (*corremos*) and they or you all run (*corren*). It's worth investing in a good Spanish verb book, such as the Collins series, because this will explain everything you need to know about the different types of verbs and how they change.

On the topic of verbs, you need to know that, in Spanish, there are two verbs meaning 'to be' – *ser* and *estar*. You need to be clear which verb to use in specific situations, because if you can't differentiate between them, your Spanish learning journey will be much more difficult.

Briefly, use *ser* for permanent states and occupations, and *estar* for temporary states and geographical locations. So you would say Soy enfermera (I am a nurse), but *Estoy feliz.* (I am happy). You are trained as a nurse, so it's your occupation, but your happiness could change to sadness some time soon. It's worth reading up on the use of these two verbs before you get too immersed in vocabulary.

PERSONAL PRONOUNS

As you probably noticed from the above explanation, you don't need to say ‚you run' in Spanish (*tú corres*); instead, you can just say *corres*. However, you need to know the different pronouns, and how to use them in sentences and conversation.

	Singular	Formal	Plural	Formal
1st person	I	"	We	"
1º persona	Yo	"	Nosotros/as	"
2nd person	You	"	You	"
2º persona	Tú/vos	Usted	Vosotros/as	Ustedes
3rd person	He, she, it	"	They	"
3º persona	Él, ella, ello	"	Ellos, Ellas	"

SINGULAR AND PLURAL

Just like English, Spanish also has plurals for different words. Normally, you only need to add an ‚s', or ‚es'. However, if the singular ends in ‚z,' the plural form will be different. For example:

English singular	Spanish singular	English plural	Spanish plural
Girl	Niña	Girls	Niñas

English	Spanish	English Plural	Spanish Plural
Book	Libro	Books	Libros
Song	Canción	Songs	Canciones
Dog	Perro	Dogs	Perros
Car	Carro	Cars	Carros
Rice	Arroz	Rice	Arroces*
Nut	Nuez	Nuts	Nueces
Light	Luz	Lights	Luces

*Restaurants will say ‗los arroces' to describe their rice dishes on the menu.

CAPITALIZATION

Although this is not important in speaking Spanish, you should be aware that some of the capitalization rules that exist in English don't apply in Spanish. For instance, days of the week, nationalities, months, and languages don't need to be capitalized when you are writing in Spanish. However, countries do. You might say ‚Hablo español' (I speak Spanish), but you would say ‚Soy de España.' (I am from Spain).

These are the main points where Spanish differs from English, and it may take a while to get used to them. However, you'll be surprised how quickly you'll get into the habit of using the correct grammar variations – all it takes is a bit of research and lots of practice!

CHAPTER FOUR

BASIC GENERAL WORDS AND PHRASES

Greetings form an important component of any conversation, in any language. In this chapter, we will talk about greetings, courteous words, wishing people happy holidays and much more.

Also, you'll learn the correct vocabulary for questions, and basic conversations, and how to use formal and informal modes of address.

GREETINGS

English	Spanish neutral	Spanish formal	Spanish informal
Welcome	Bienvenido		
Hello	¡Hola!		
Thank you	Gracias		
Goodbye	Adiós		
Hello (phone)	¿Aló?		
How are you?		¿Cómo está usted?	¿Cómo estás?

COURTESY

English	Spanish
Good bye	Adiós
See you soon	Hasta luego
See you later	Te veo luego, Hasta luego
Take care	Cuídate
See you tomorrow	Te veo mañana, Hasta mañana

English	Spanish
Good luck	¡Buena suerte!
Cheers	¡Salud!
Have a good meal	¡Buen provecho!
Good morning	Buenos días
Good afternoon	Buenas tardes
Good night	Buenas noches
Have a nice day!	¡Que pase un buen día!
Have a nice trip!	¡Buen viaje!
I love you	Te quiero, Te amo
Excuse me	Disculpe/ Permiso

Here is a helpful YouTube video to boost your pronunciation/accent:

https://www.youtube.com/watch?v=m9eaWTKrBDk [YouTube search: Basic Conversation in Spanish - Greetings and Goodbyes].

HOLIDAYS AND SPECIAL OCCASIONS

English	**Spanish**
Merry Christmas!	¡Feliz navidad!
Happy New Year!	¡Feliz año nuevo!

English	Spanish
Happy Easter!	¡Felices pascuas!
Happy birthday!	¡Feliz cumpleaños!
Happy Valentine's day!	¡Feliz día de San Valentín!
Happy Mother's Day!	¡Feliz día de la madre!
Happy Father's Day!	¡Feliz día del padre!

INTRODUCING YOURSELF

English	Neutral	Informal	Formal
What's your name?		¿Cómo te llamas?	¿Cómo se llama usted?
Good, thank you, and you?		Bien gracias, ¿y tú?	Bien gracias, ¿y usted?
Long time no see.	¡Tanto tiempo sin verte!		
My name is—	Mi nombre es—		
Where are you from?		¿De dónde eres?	¿De dónde es usted?
I am from—	Yo soy de—		
Pleased to meet you.	Mucho gusto en conocerte		
Nice to see you!		¡Qué agradable verte!	¡Qué agradable verlo!

SIMPLE QUESTIONS

English	Spanish
Who?	¿Quién?
Where	¿Dónde?
When	¿Cuándo?
Why	¿Por qué?
How?	¿Cómo?
Whom?	¿Quién?

RESPONSES AND COMMON QUESTIONS

English	Neutral	Formal	Informal
I don't know	No sé, No lo sé		
I understand	Entiendo		
I don't understand	No entiendo		
Do you speak English?		¿Habla inglés?	¿Hablas inglés?
Do you speak Spanish?		¿Habla español?	¿Hablas español?
Yes, a little	Sí, un poco		

How do you say—? ¿Cómo se dice—en español?

How much is it? ¿Cuánto cuesta?

Sorry ¡Perdón!, ¡Lo siento!

Where is the toilet? ¿Dónde están los sanitarios?

Where is the restroom? ¿Dónde están los baños?

How do I get to—? ¿Cómo llego a—?

Where's a phone booth? ¿Dónde están los teléfonos públicos?

Do you have Wi-Fi? ¿Tienen wifi?

Do you have change for a dollar? ¿Tiene cambio para un billete de un dólar?

SIMPLE EMERGENCY WORDS

English	Neutral	Formal
Informal		
Help!	¡Ayuda!, ¡Auxilio!	
Fire!	¡Fuego!	
Stop!	¡Alto!	¡Deténgase!
¡Détente!		

Watch out!	¡Cuidado!
Be careful!	Ten cuidado!

Even if you cannot construct a sensible sentence, just blurt any of the words we have discussed above to get your message across.

Greetings form an important part of the conversation in Spain, where it is expected to say ‗Hello' and ask after someone's welfare, even if you're just being served in a store or a bank. Spanish people consider it the height of rudeness to just walk into a store and ask for what you want with no greeting.

Remember, too, to use the appropriate formal or informal greeting, because that matters as well. The informal second person (usted) is used for people you hardly know, or those who are professionally or maybe socially superior. It's often also used as a form of respectful address for older people, so it's important to know the difference.

CHAPTER FIVE

NUMBERS

Everyday conversation will definitely involve the use of numbers. You could be buying stuff at the local store, saying how many siblings you have, talking about money, or exchanging phone numbers, but you won't be able to avoid using some numbers in Spanish. In this chapter, I will introduce you to how to say numbers in Spanish.

1 – 20

Spanish	Numeral
Cero	0
Uno	1
Dos	2
Tres	3
Cuatro	4
Cinco	5

Spanish	Numeral
Seis	6
Siete	7
Ocho	8
Nueve	9
Diez	10
Once	11
Doce	12
Trece	13
Catorce	14
Quince	15
Dieciséis	16
Diecisiete	17
Dieciocho	18
Diecinueve	19
Veinte	20

21 – 100

Spanish	Numeral

Veintiuno	21
Veintidós	22
Veintitrés	23
Veinticuatro	24
Veinticinco	25
Veintiséis	26
Veintisiete	27
Veintiocho	28
Veintinueve	29
Treinta	30
Treinta y uno	31
Treinta y dos	32
Treinta y tres	33
Treinta y cuatro	34
Treinta y cinco	35
Treinta y seis	36

Treinta y siete	37
Treinta y ocho	38
Treinta y nueve	39
Cuarenta	40
Cincuenta	50
Sesenta	60
Setenta	70
Ochenta	80
Noventa	90
Cien	100

As you see from the above, from 16-19, you just need to know how to say 10 and 6, i.e., *dieciseis*, 10 and 7, i.e., *diecisiete*, and on up to 19 which is 10 and 9. The same pattern is followed from 21-29, i.e., *veinti* + number as just one word. For instance, 21=*veintiuno* then 22=*veintidós* then 23= *veintitrés*. The same pattern follows in 31-39, i.e., *treinta* followed by the number as two words *treinta uno, treinta dos, treinta tres*. From 50 to 100 it's practically the same: *y uno, y dos, y tres,* etc. If you are saying anything between 101 and 199, you simply need to say *ciento* followed by the number.

100 – 1,000

Spanish	Numeral
Cien	100
Doscientos	200
Trescientos	300
Cuatrocientos	400
Quinientos	500
Seiscientos	600
Setecientos	700
Ochocientos	800
Novecientos	900
Mil	1,000

Again, if you want to speak like the native Spanish speakers do, you can watch a couple of YouTube videos: https://www.youtube.com/watch?v=27KsV2MUKGU [YouTube search: Spanish Numbers From 1 -100] and https://www.youtube.com/watch?v=qJ93x5PMMko [YouTube search: Learn Spanish - Count from 0 to 100!].

TELLING THE TIME

English	Spanish
What time is it?	¿Qué hora es?

I don't have a watch	No tengo reloj
I don't know the hour	No sé la hora
It's twelve o'clock	Son las doce en punto
It's five past one	Es la una y cinco
It's ten past two	Son las dos y diez
It's quarter past three	Son las tres y cuarto
It's twenty past four	Son las cuatro y veinte
It's twenty-five past five	Son las cinco y veinticinco
It's half past six	Son las seis y media
It's twenty-five to seven	Son veinticinco para las siete
It's twenty to eight	Son veinte para las ocho
It's quarter to nine	Son cuarto para las nueve
It's ten to ten	Son diez para las diez
It's five to eleven	Son cinco para las once
It's 15:00	Son las tres de la tarde
It's 21:15	Son las nueve y cuarto
It's 16:50	Son las cinco menos diez

It's 13:40   Son las dos menos veinte

As you can see, when adding minutes, you just need to add y. For instance, 6.05 is *seis y cinco*.

On the other hand, if you want to say ―x‖ minutes to the hour, here is how to go about it.

To say 10 minutes to five in Spanish, you say *son las cinco menoz diez*.

DAYS OF THE WEEK

English	Spanish
Monday	Lunes
Tuesday	Martes
Wednesday	Miércoles
Thursday	Jueves
Friday	Viernes
Saturday	Sábado
Sunday	Domingo

You can get more pronunciation help from this YouTube video: https://www.youtube.com/watch?v=tCV9ba-mfm0 [YouTube search: 01008 Spanish Lesson - Days of the Week].

MONTHS

English	Spanish
January	Enero
February	Febrero
March	Marzo
April	Abril
May	Mayo
June	Junio
July	Julio
August	Agosto
September	Septiembre
October	Octubre
November	Noviembre
December	Diciembre

SEASONS

English	Spanish
Winter	Invierno
Spring	Primavera
Summer	Verano

Autumn   Otoño

Here are a couple of great YouTube videos to help you pronounce the above: https://www.youtube.com/watch?v=D_ctUMy9v6w [YouTube search: Seasons and months in Spanish] and https://www.youtube.com/watch?v=DLN8-PZwUZ4 [YouTube search: How to say the days of the week in spanish .mp4].

WEATHER

English	Spanish
Blustery	Borrascoso
Breeze / a sea breeze	Brisa / una brisa marina
Thunderclap	Trueno
Clear sky/day	Cielo/día despejado
Climate	El clima
Cloudburst	Chaparrón, un aguacero
Clouds	Nubes
Cold	El frío
Damp	Húmedo
Degree	Grado

English	Spanish
Dew	El rocío
Drizzle	Chispeando/ lloviznar
Flash of lightning	Relámpago
Flood	Inundación
Fog	Niebla
Forked lightning	Una culebrina
Frost	Escarcha/ helar
Frosty night	Noche de helada
Gale	Viento fuerte, una vendaval
Gust of wind	Racha
Hail	Granizar
Hailstones	Las piedras de granizo /los granizos
Hailstorm	Granizada
Haziness	Lo neblinoso, la nebulosidad
He was struck by lightning	Le cayó un rayo
Heat wave	Ola de calor
High	Alto

Humid	Húmedo
Humidity	Humedad
Hurricane	Un huracán
Ice	El hielo
It's clear	Está despejado
It's cloudy	Está nublado
It's cold	Está frío
It's cool	Está fresco
It's raining	Está lloviendo
It's snowing	Está nevando
It's sunny	Está soleado
It's warm	Está caluroso
It's hailing	Hay granizo
It's hot	Hace calor
It's nice out	Hace buen tiempo
Lightning	Relámpago

Low	Bajo
Moon	La luna
Rain	Lluvia
Rain shower	El chubasco
Sky	El cielo
Snow	Nieve
Snowball	Bola de nieve
Star	La estrella
Storm	Un temporal, tormenta
Stormy day	Día tormentoso
Streak of lightning	Rayo
Sun	El sol
Sunny day	Día soleado
Sunny spell	Claro
Sunset	El atardecer
Temperature	La temperatura

Thaw	Deshielo/ deshelar
The humidity is very high.	La humedad está muy alta.
The temperature is -10 degrees.	La temperatura está a menos diez grados.
The weather is bad.	Hace mal tiempo.
The weather is good.	Hace buen tiempo.
There's fog.	Hay neblina.
There's a windstorm.	Hay un vendaval.
Thunder	Los truenos
Thundercloud	Nubarrón
Thunderstorm	La tormenta
Tide	La mareada
To become muggy	Abochornarse
To clear up	Despejar
Today is a rainy day.	Hoy es un día de lluvia.
Today is a sunny day.	Hoy es un día soleado.
Tomorrow will be a sunny day.	Mañana será un día soleado.

Turbulence	La turbulencia
TV weather report	Tiempo TV
Very hard rain	Esta chorreando
Weather	El tiempo (climatológico)
Weatherman	El hombre del tiempo (climatológico)
What's the weather like?	¿Qué tiempo hace?
Wind	Viento
Yesterday was partially cloudy.	Ayer estaba parcialmente nublado.
Rainbow	El arco iris

COLORS

English	Spanish
Red	Rojo
Yellow	Amarillo
Orange	Anaranjado, Naranja
Purple	Morado
Blue	Azul

Brown   Café, Marrón

Black   Negro

Grey   Gris

White   Blanco

Pink   Rosado

Here is a YouTube video that will greatly help you in your pronunciation: https://www.youtube.com/watch?v=H15nDRfnfWo [YouTube search: Spanish vocabulary - Learn Spanish Colors in Less than 5 minutes]. Another great video is https://www.youtube.com/watch?v=-jf5WnqcePQ [YouTube search: Learn the colors in Spanish with BASHO & FRIENDS [Episode Version]].

ANIMALS

English	Spanish
Wolf	El Lobo
Wing	El Ala (F)
Whale	La Ballena
Weasel	La Comadreja
Wasp	La Avispa

Turtle	La Tortuga
Turkey	El Pavo
Tuna	El Atún
Trout	La Trucha
Toad	El Sapo
Tiger	El Tigre
Tail	La Cola
Tadpole	El Renacuajo
Swan	El Cisne
Swallow	La Golondrina
Stork	La Cigüeña
Starfish	La Estrella De Mar
Squirrel	La Ardilla
Squid	El Calamar
Spider	La Araña
Sparrow	El Gorrión

Sole	El Lenguado
Snake	La Serpiente / La Culebra
Snail	El Caracol
Slug	La Babosa
Skin	La Piel
Shrimp	La Gamba
Sheep	La Oveja
Shark	El Tiburón
Seal	La Foca
Seahorse	El Caballito De Mar
Sea Gull	La Gaviota
Scorpion	El Escorpión
Scale	La Escama
Salmon	El Salmón
Rooster	El Gallo
Rat	La Rata

Raccoon	El Mapache
Rabbit	El Conejo
Pony	El Potro
Pike	El Sollo
Pigeon	El Pichón
Pig	El Cerdo
Penguin	El Pingüino
Paw	La Pata
Partridge	La Perdiz
Parrot	El Loro
Oyster	La Ostra
Ox	El Buey
Owl	El Búho
Ostrich	El Avestruz
Octopus	El Pulpo
Nightingale	El Ruiseñor

Nest	El Nido
Mussel	El Mejillón
Mule	El Mulo
Mouse	El Ratón
Moth	La Polilla
Mosquito	El Mosquito
Monkey	El Mono
Mole	El Topo
Mackerel	La Caballa
Louse	El Piojo
Lobster	La Langosta
Lizard	El Lagarto
Antelope	El Antílope
Ant	La Hormiga
Lion	El León
Lark	La Alondra

Kitten	El Gatito
Jellyfish	La Medusa
Insect	El Insecto
Iguana	La Iguana
Hummingbird	El Colibrí
Horse	El Caballo
Horn	El Cuerno
Hoof	La Pezuña
Herring	El Arenque
Heron	La Garza
Hen	La Gallina
Hedgehog	El Erizo
Hare	La Liebre
Hamster	La Marmota
Grasshopper	El Saltamontes
Cheetah	El Guepardo
Caterpillar	La Oruga

Cat	El Gato
Carp	La Carpa
Calf	El Ternero
Butterfly	La Mariposa
Bull	El Toro
Blackbird	El Mirlo
Bird	El Pájaro
Beetle	El Escarabajo
Bee	La Abeja
Bear	El Oso
Beak	El Pico
Gorilla	El Gorila
Goose	El Ganso
Goat	La Cabra
Giraffe	La Jirafa
Gill	La Branquia

Fur	El Pelo
Frog	La Rana
Fox	El Zorro
Fly	La Mosca
Flea	La Pulga
Fish	El Pez
Fin	La Aleta
Feather	La Pluma
Elephant	El Elefante
Egg	El Huevo
Eel	La Anguila
Eagle	El Águila (F)
Duck	El Pato
Dragonfly	La Libélula
Donkey	El Burro
Dog	El Perro

Deer	El Ciervo
Crow	El Cuervo
Crocodile	El Cocodrilo
Crayfish	El Cangrejo (de río)
Crab	El Cangrejo
Cow	La Vaca
Cod	El Bacalao
Cocoon	El Capullo
Cockroach	La Cucaracha
Claw	La Zarpa
Chimpanzee	El Chimpancé
Chicken	El Pollo
Bat	El Murciélago
Badger	El Tejón
Antler	El Asta
Antenna	La Antena

Here are a few YouTube videos to help you with the pronunciations:

- https://www.youtube.com/watch?v=0qdlMipcsWQ
    - [YouTube search: Animal names in Spanish with BASHO & FRIENDS – Animales]

- https://www.youtube.com/watch?v=-qj4Pa-sBCA
    - [YouTube search: Spanish lesson 97: Animals names – Animales]

- https://www.youtube.com/watch?v=-8F6Rkhj6wo
    - [YouTube search: Animals names in Spanish part 3 Spanish For Beginners]

- https://www.youtube.com/watch?v=QeR8PjmttlU
    - [YouTube search: Animals names in Spanish part 4 Spanish For Beginners]

- https://www.youtube.com/watch?v=AgJxOV0jY90
    - [YouTube search: Animals names in Spanish part 2 Spanish For Beginners]

While some of the vocabulary in this chapter may not seem to be associated with numbers, as was stated at the beginning of the chapter, numbers are used a lot in Spanish.

You'll be surprised how many of the words here are used in conjunction with numbers.

CHAPTER SIX

FAMILY AND FRIENDS

If you spend any time at all in Spain or any Spanish speaking country, it won't be long before you realize just how important the family and family life is. Go to the beach on a Sunday in summer, and you're likely to see tables spread out under the shade of the palm trees with several generations of the same family enjoying good food and each other's company. And when you're speaking with Spanish people, they're bound to ask about your *familia* (family), so you really need this vocabulary!

VOCABULARY

English	Spanish
Mother	Madre
Father	Padre
Son	Hijo
Daughter	Hija
Grandmother	Abuela

English	Spanish
Grandfather	Abuelo
Grandchild	Nieto
Grandaughter	Nieta
Brother	Hermano
Sister	Hermana
Aunt	Tía
Uncle	Tío
Cousin	Primo/a
Niece	Sobrina
Nephew	Sobrino
Married	Casado/a
Friend	Amigo/a
Husband	Esposo
Wife	Esposa
Divorced	Divorciado/a
Sister-in-law	Cuñada

English	Spanish
Brother-in-law	Cuñado
Father-in law	Suegro
Mother-in-law	Suegra
Daughter-in-law	Nuera
Son-in-law	Yerno
Orphan	Huérfano/a
Parents	Padres
Babysitter	Niñera
Siblings	Hermanos
Stepmother	Madrastra
Stepchild	Hijastro
Stepfather	Padrastro
Widow	Viuda
Widower	Viudo
Adopted	Adoptado/a

This YouTube video should help you in your pronunciation and jog your mind so that you can remember what to say when speaking the language: https://www.youtube.com/watch?v=iITu7S-8cLo [YouTube search: How to say Mother in Spanish - and father, sister, brother, grandfather ...].

PHRASES
English **Spanish**

My sister will get married.	Mi hermana se casará.
My parents will get divorced.	Mis padres se divorciarán.
My aunt is a widow.	Mi tía es viuda.
I don't like my stepmother.	No me agrada mi madrastra.
My cousin is a nice person.	Mi primo es una buena persona.
My mother-in-law hates me.	Mi suegra me odia.
My stepfather doesn't get along with me.	Mi padrastro no se lleva bien conmigo.
I love my best friend.	Amo a mi mejor amigo.
When will they get divorce?	¿Cuándo se divorciarán?
Who knows.	Quién sabe.
Aunt Lila always sends me money.	Mi tía Lila siempre me manda dinero.
The babysitter will take care of my son today.	La niñera cuidará de mi hijo hoy.

My brother realized he's adopted.   Mi hermano se dio cuenta que es adoptado.

My uncle's wife died.   La esposa de mi tío murió.

My grandfather will travel with me.   Mi abuelo viajará conmigo.

MEETING NEW PEOPLE

English	Spanish
Hello	Hola
What's your name?	¿Cuál es tu nombre?
My name is—	Mi nombre es—
Where are you from?	¿De dónde eres?
I'm from—	Soy de—
Nice to meet you	Encantado/a de conocerte
I am—years old	Tengo—años
How old are you?	¿Cuántos años tienes?
Let me introduce you to—	Te presento a—
Are you married?	¿Estás casado/a?
She is my wife	Ella es mi esposa

He is my husband — Él es mi esposo
She is my mother — Ella es mi madre

My sister will get married — Mi hermana se casará

Do you have children? — ¿Tienes hijos?

Where are you staying? — ¿En dónde te hospedas?

I don't speak Spanish — No hablo español

Would you like to—? — ¿Te gustaría—?

Go for a walk — Dar un paseo

What does—mean? — ¿Qué significa—?

I am studying Spanish — Estoy estudiando español

What's your telephone number? — ¿Cuál es tu número de teléfono?

What's your address? — ¿Cuál es tu dirección?

I hope to see you soon — Espero verte pronto

Here is a great YouTube video that will help you master the pronunciation and even expand your vocabulary: https://www.youtube.com/watch?v=H-84u9D3Qpc [YouTube search: Spanish greetings and farewells for simple conversations].

NATIONALITY

English Country/Demonym	Spanish
País/Gentilicio	
Australia/Australian	Australia/Australiano
Bolivia/Bolivian	Bolivia/Boliviano
Austria/Austrian	Austria/Austriaco
Belgium/Belgian	Bélgica/Bélgico
Brazil/Brazilian	Brasil/Brasileño
Canada/Canadian	Canadá/Canadiense
Egypt/Egyptian	Egipto/Egipcio
Hungary/Hungarian	Húngaria/Húngaro
Peru/Peruvian	Perú/Peruano
India/Indian	India/Indiano
Iran/Iranian	Irán/Irani
Italy/Italian	Italia/Italiano
Norway/Norwegian	Noruega/Noruego
Colombia/Colombian	Colombia/Colombiano
Russia/Russian	Rusia/Ruso

Chile/Chilean	Chile/Chileno
Cuba/Cuban	Cuba/Cubano
Germany/German	Alemania/Alemano
Jamaica/Jamaican	Jamaica/Jamaicano
Korea/Korean	Korea/Koreano
Mexico/Mexican	México/Mexicano
Nicaragua/Nicaraguan Nicaragua/Nicaraguense	
Paraguay/Paraguayan	Paraguay/Paraguayo
South Africa/South African	Sur África/Sudafricano
United States/American Unidos/Americano	Estados
Uruguay/Uruguayan	Uruguay/Uruguayo
Venezuela/Venezuelan	Venezuela/Venezolano
China/Chinese	China/Chino
Japan/Japanese	Japón/Japonés
France/French	Francia/Francés

Note: Change the final ‗o' to ‗a' for females.

This YouTube video will come in handy to build your pronunciation and accent: https://www.youtube.com/watch?v=WzE0H5T1Ddc [YouTube search: Countries and nationalities in Spanish: list, sentences & questions].

Phrases

English	Spanish
I'm from France	Soy de Francia
Where are you from?	¿De dónde eres?
You are Spanish	Tú eres español
How's your country?	¿Cómo es tu país?
It's a nice country	Es un país bonito
My best friend is Chinese.	Mi major amigo es chino.
My roommate wants to go to—	Mi compañero de cuarto quiere viajar a—
What language do you speak in your country?	¿Qué idioma hablas en tu país?

Note: It is optional to use the articles *el, la, los* and *las* before many countries in Spanish unless the particular name has such an article, e.g., El Salvador.

Speaking about your family and your country is important in Spanish conversation, because the Spanish are naturally curious people, and they want to know all about you, and where you are from. Many Spanish people these days are also surprisingly well traveled, so they will be keen to tell you about their adventures in foreign lands.

CHAPTER SEVEN

MOVING AROUND

If you're traveling to Spain – or anywhere in Spain – you're going

to need to travel by plane, train, automobile, bus or boat, and this chapter will help you to do that painlessly. One big advantage of speaking the language of the country you're

traveling in is that you don't automatically stand out as a tourist, and therefore you're less likely to attract the attention of the particularly nasty breed of person who preys on tourists by stealing from them or scamming them. Here's all you need to move around safely and confidently in Spain.

AT THE AIRPORT

Vocabulary

English	Spanish
Suitcase	Maleta
Luggage	Equipaje
Ticket	Boleto

English	Spanish
Security guard	Guardia de seguridad
Metal detector	Detector de metales
Conveyor belt	Banda
Baggage cart	Carrito de equipaje
Porter	Maletero
Non-smoking section	Sección de no fumar
Passport	Pasaporte
Baggage claim ticket	Talón
Carry-on bag	Maletín
Stewardess	Azafata
Belt	Cinturón
Exit door	Puerta de emergencia
Seat	Asiento
Customs office	Aduana
Luggage claim area	Área de reclamo de equipaje
Boarding pass	Pase de abordaje

Flight attendant　　　　Sobrecargo

Luggage compartment　　Compartimiento de equipaje

Aisle　　　　　　　　　Pasillo

Terminal building　　　Terminal

Runway　　　　　　　　Pista

Flight　　　　　　　　　Vuelo

Wing　　　　　　　　　Ala

Tail　　　　　　　　　　Cola

Captain　　　　　　　　Capitán

Seat　　　　　　　　　Asiento

Delay　　　　　　　　　Retraso

Window　　　　　　　　Ventanilla

Passenger　　　　　　　Pasajero

Phrases
English　　　　　　　**Spanish**

Flight number　　　　　Número de vuelo

Departure time　　　　Hora de salida

Arrival time	Hora de llegada
Boarding time	Hora de embarque
We have arrived	Hemos aterrizado
Seat belt on	Mantenga el cinturón puesto
Turbulence zone	Zona de turbulencia
What terminal are you looking for?	¿Qué terminal está buscando usted?
I'm looking for terminal E	Estoy buscando la terminal E
Where are you headed?	¿Hacia dónde se dirige?
I am going to—	Voy a—
Terminal E is for international flights	La terminal E es para vuelos internacionales
Where is customs?	¿Dónde está aduanas?
Could I see your luggage claim ticket?	¿Podría ver su talón?
How many bags do you have?	Cuántas maletas tiene?
I want to reserve two seats to Spain.	Me gustaría reservar dos asientos para España.

How much is a round trip ticket? ¿Cuánto cuesta un boleto ida y vuelta?

How much is a one-way ticket? ¿Cuánto cuesta un boleto de ida/vuelta?

Will you pay by cash or by credit card? ¿Pagará con efectivo o con tarjeta de crédito?

Can I see your ticket and passport? ¿Podría ver su boleto y su pasaporte?

Thanks. Where do I go next? Gracias. ¿A dónde voy ahora?

Fill out this form before the plane lands. Llene este formulario antes de que aterrice el avión.

I had a good trip. Thanks for your help. Tuve un buen viaje. Gracias por su ayuda.

Do you have anything to declare? ¿Tiene algo que declarar?

I just have a perfume. Solo tengo un perfume.

Excuse me, where is the exit? Disculpe, ¿dónde está la salida?

Excuse me, where is the cafeteria? Disculpe, ¿dónde está la cafetería?

Here is a great YouTube video that will help in building your accent: https://www.youtube.com/watch?v=OA1Im6Sq_ps [YouTube search: Learn Spanish Online - At the Airport]. You can also watch/listen to another useful video here: https://www.youtube.com/watch?v=Y7MEdUBxJQc [YouTube search: Airport Spanish vocab].

ASKING FOR DIRECTIONS

English	Spanish
Right	Derecha
Left	Izquierda
Road map	Mapa
Street map	Plano
Street/Road	Calle
Avenue	Avenida
Boulevard	Bulevar, Alameda
Alley	Callejón
Pavement	Acera

Shortcut	Atajo
Highway	Autopista
Lane	Carril
Exit	Salida
Traffic light	Semáforo
Crossroads	Cruce
North	Norte
Sur	South
East	Este
West	Oeste
Near	Cerca
Go up	Sube
Opposite	Enfrente
Roundabout	Rotonda, Glorieta
Behind	Detrás

This YouTube video will help you greatly when asking for directions in Spanish:

https://www.youtube.com/watch?v=GQRlO6tXLgg   [YouTube search: Basic Spanish | Lesson 24 | Asking for Directions].

MEANS OF TRANSPORT

English	Spanish
On foot	A pie
Bicycle	Bicicleta
Car	Carro, Coche
Bus	Bus
Motorbike	Moto
Boat	Bote
Plane	Avión
Train	Tren
Van	Furgoneta

PLACES

Vocabulary

English	Spanish
Shops	Tiendas
Shopping mall	Centro commercial
Art gallery	Galería de arte
Park	Parque

English	Spanish
Parking	Parqueo
Historic Center	Centro histórico
Museum	Museo
Market	Mercado
Supermarket	Supermercado
House	Casa
Hotel	Hotel
Apartment	Apartamento
Central park	Parque central
Airport	Aeropuerto
Bookstore	Librería
Hospital	Hospital
Pharmacy	Farmacia
Bar	Bar
Bank	Banco
Beach	Playa

Phrases

English	Spanish
Excuse me, where is the north tower?	Disculpe, ¿dónde está la torre norte?
Is it far?	¿Está lejos?
I am lost	Estoy perdido
Could you show me on a map?	¿Me podría enseñar en el mapa?
I am looking for the central park	Estoy buscando el parque central
Is there a restaurant near here?	¿Hay un restaurant cerca de aquí?
How do I get to___?	¿Cómo llego a___?
Is there any bus that goes nearby?	¿Hay algún bus que pase cerca?
Go straight on	Siga recto
Turn left	Gire a la izquierda
Turn the corner	Doble la esquina
I'll go on foot	Me iré a pie
Turn around	Dé la vuelta

English	Spanish
Cross the street	Cruce la calle
It's on the other side of the street	Está del otro lado de la calle
It's at the end of the road	Está al final de la calle
It's ten minutes away	Está a diez minutos
Take the next left	Tome la próxima izquierda
Take the second road	Tome la siguiente carretera
Here behind	Aquí al lado
I will go for a stroll	Iré por un paseo
Could you show me the route please?	¿Me podría mostrar el itinerario, por favor?
Can I buy a map here?	¿Puedo comprar un mapa aquí?
Is the bus delayed?	¿Está retrasado el autobús?
I missed the train	Perdí el tren.
Where are you heading?	¿Hacia dónde se dirige?
Will I have to change buses?	¿Tendré que cambiar de autobuse?
Is this the bus to Chicago?	¿Es este el autobús para Chicago?

English	Spanish
Where is the next stop?	¿Dónde es la próxima parada?
Do I have to get off here?	¿Tengo que bajarme aquí?
Excuse me, where is the museum?	Disculpe, ¿dónde está el museo?
Where is the bus stop?	¿Dónde está la parada del autobús?
What's the train schedule?	¿Cuál es el horario del tren?
Do you have GPS on your phone?	¿Tienes GPS en tu celular?
What's the name of the street?	¿Cuál es el nombre de la calle?
How far from here is it?	¿Qué tan lejos de aquí está eso?
Do you know any shortcut?	¿Sabes algún atajo?
Where is Jack's bar?	¿Dónde está el bar de Jack's?
How long is the trip?	¿Qué tan largo es el viaje?
Watch your things	Cuida tus cosas
Your backpack is too heavy	Tu mochila es muy pesada
Carry on for ten minutes	Sigue durante diez minutos
Take the third exit at the roundabout.	Cuando llegues a la rotonda, toma la tercera salida.

Excuse me, where is the pharmacy?   Disculpe, ¿dónde está la farmacia?

You can watch this YouTube video to help you in your accent and pronunciation: https://www.youtube.com/watch?v=3ifyku_6dxA   [YouTube search: Asking and giving directions in Spanish - Direcciones en español].

Note: From this point forward, I will purposely leave out pronunciations in Spanish so you can practice searching for them on your own. Simply go to YouTube and search —How to speak Spanish at the…‖ or —How to… in Spanish‖. If you find yourself struggling with pronunciations or simply want to make your Spanish accent sound more like the native speakers, the videos will come in handy.

AT THE BEACH

If you want to speak Spanish at the beach, this part will provide you with the vocabulary you need. If you have been following this guide and checking out the videos, your accent should be a lot better now. As such, I will purposely not include the pronunciations for this part (you can consider this a sort of assignment). *Vocabulary*

English	Spanish
Beach	Playa
Sea	Mar

English	Spanish
Sunblock	Bloqueador solar
Sun glasses	Gafas de sol
Sand	Arena
Wave	Ola
Towel	Toalla
Umbrella	Sombrilla
Castle	Castillo
Lifeguard	Salvavidas
Drown	Ahogar
Bronzer	Bronceador
Bikini	Bikini
Bathing suit	Traje de baño
Swim	Nadar
Shadow	Sombra
Ice cream	Helado
Sun	Sol
Tan	Bronceado

English	Spanish
Sun burn	Quemado
Sandals	Sandalias
Low tide	Marea baja
High tide	Marea alta

Phrases

English	**Spanish**
Could you put some sunblock on me?	¿Me podrías poner un poco de bloqueador?

Could you get in the shade, please? ¿Te podrías poner debajo de la sombra, por favor?

Where is the lifeguard? ¿Dónde está el salvavidas?

The sand is hot. Be careful please! La arena está caliente. ¡Ten cuidado por favor!

My son wants to build a sand castle. Mi hijo quiere construir un castillo de arena.

I want to get a tan today Hoy me quiero broncear.

Let's eat ice cream Comamos un helado.

Is it safe to swim in the sea? ¿Es seguro nadar en el mar?

I like your bathing suit, it's very chic. Me gusta tu traje de baño, está de moda.

How long will we stay at the beach? ¿Cuánto tiempo nos quedaremos en la playa?

Do you know if the tide is high? ¿Sabes si la marea está alta?

Don't go too far; you could drown. No te vayas tan lejos porque te podrías ahogar.

Put a towel on the sand before you sit.   Pon una toalla en la arena antes de que te sientes.

Do you have my sunglasses?   ¿Tienes mis gafas de sol?

When will the tide go out?   ¿A qué hora baja la marea?

Is the sun is very strong right now?   ¿Sabes si el sol está muy fuerte a esta hora?

I want to eat ice cream. It's too hot here.   Quiero comer un helado. Está muy caluroso aquí.

I love the beach because it's peaceful.   Amo la playa porque me da paz.

Where should we sunbathe?   ¿Dónde deberíamos tomar el sol?

Did you bring a book to read?   ¿Trajiste un libro para leer?

I like to read at the beach.   A mí me gusta leer en la playa.   Did you bring the beer?   ¿Trajiste las cervezas?

    Again, if you can speak Spanish on the beach, you are less likely to present a target to thieves. It's also a great opportunity to listen to Spanish people speaking without appearing too obvious, and that will help your pronunciation enormously.

CHAPTER EIGHT

FOOD, COOKING AND RESTAURANTS

Food and cooking plays a big part in life in Spain. Typical Spanish cuisine is simple but tasty, with just a few quality ingredients combined to make a hearty meal. Practice your Spanish by buying fruit and vegetables at the street markets – you'll be offered lots of samples, because the Spanish are justly proud of their produce! And try your hand at cooking some authentic Spanish dishes. Reading a recipe in Spanish is a great way to expand your vocabulary and fill your stomach at the same time!

FRUITS

English	Spanish
Apple	Manzana
Banana	Banano
Apricot	Albaricoque

English	Spanish
Coconut	Coco
Blackberry	Mora
Grape	Uva
Kiwi	Kiwi
Lemon	Limón
Mandarin	Mandarina
Mango	Mango
Nectarine	Nectarina
Fig	Higo
Orange	Naranja
Peach	Durazno, Melocotón
Pineapple	Piña
Plum	Ciruela
Raspberry	Frambuesa
Watermelon	Sandía
Melon	Melón
Lime	Lima

Cherry   Cereza

This YouTube video should help you pronounce the words a lot better: https://www.youtube.com/watch?v=HsVzzg35aTU [YouTube search: Fruits Vocabulary English-Spanish]. Another great video is https://www.youtube.com/watch?v=VBZKehbu9ug [YouTube search: Spanish/English: Fruit Vocabulary].

VEGETABLES

English	Spanish
Carrot	Zanahoria
Asparagus	Espárrago
Avocado	Aguacate
Broccoli	Brócoli
Cabbage	Repollo
Beet	Remolacha
Corn	Maíz
Cucumber	Pepino
Lechuga	Lettuce
Celery	Apio

Eggplant	Berenjena
Garlic	Ajo
Ginger	Jengibre
Mushroom	Champiñón
Onion	Cebolla
Parsley	Perejil
Potato	Papa/patata
Pumpkin	Calabaza

The following two videos take different approaches that will help you greatly in your pronunciation: https://www.youtube.com/watch?v=qtWs49YjOAg [YouTube search: LAS VERDURAS Y SUS NOMBRES - THE NAME OF VEGETABLES IN SPANISH - ESPAÑOL PARA TODOS] and https://www.youtube.com/watch?v=CyeEli-Zv_Q [YouTube search: Learn Spanish - How to say Vegetable Names in Spanish].

MEATS

English	Spanish
Beef	Carne de res
Pork	Carne de cerdo

English	Spanish
Chicken	Pollo
Fish	Pescado
Shellfish	Mariscos
Ground beef	Carne molida
Roasted	Asado/rostizado
Steak	Bisté, Bistec
Sausage	Chorizo
Bacon	Tocino
Ham	Jamón
Turkey	Pavo
Duck	Pato
Lobster	Langosta
Shrimp	Camarones
Clams	Almejas

DAIRY

English	Spanish
Eggs	Huevos

Milk	Leche
Butter	Mantequilla
Cheese	Queso
Yoghurt	Yogur
Parmesan cheese	Queso parmesano

Drinks

English	Spanish
Beer	Cerveza
Coffee	Café
Wine	Vino
Juice	Jugo
Soft drink	Refresco
Tea	Té
Water	Agua

Phrases & cooking instructions

English	Spanish
How much of this?	¿Cuánto de esto?
It's $7.00	Son siete dólares

Add two tablespoons	Agrega dos cucharadas
Add a cup of sugar	Agrega una taza de azúcar
Mix all the ingredients	Mezcla todos los ingredientes
Put them all in a frying pan	Póngalos todos en el sartén
Bring it to a boil	Póngalo a hervir
Put the potatoes to fry	Ponga las papas a freír
Put the cake to bake	Ponga el pastel al horno
Leave it for five minutes until it boils	Déjelo por cinco minutos hasta que hierva
May I have a glass of water?	¿Podría darme un vaso con agua?
I'll make a salad	Haré una ensalada
Is it sweet?	¿Es dulce?
How does it taste?	¿A qué sabe?
Do you have all the ingredients?	¿Tienes todos los ingredientes?
What's missing?	¿Qué te hace falta?
Add some salt to the soup	Agrega un poco de sal a la sopa
It's time to take tea	Es hora de de tomar el té.

Serve the table — Sirve la mesa

I need two hours for cooking — Necesito dos horas para cocinar

We should make lasagna tonight. Deberíamos hacer lasaña esta noche.

How many guests do we have? ¿Cuántos invitados tenemos?

Put some fruit on the table — Pon un poco de fruta en la mesa

What do I need to make a hamburger? ¿Cuáles son los ingredientes para preparar una hamburguesa?

AT A RESTAURANT

Basic restaurant concepts

English	Spanish
Restaurant	Restaurante
Fast food restaurant	Restaurante de comida rápida
Cafeteria	Cafetería
Meal	Comida
Menu	Menú
Kitchen	Cocina
Chef	Chef

Manager	Gerente
Good service	Buen servicio
Bad service	Mal servicio
Buffet	Comida buffet
Table	Mesa
Tip	Propina
Reservation	Reservación
Cheap	Barato
Expensive	Caro
Waiter	Camarero, Mesero

Table objects

Napkin	Servilleta
Knife	Cuchillo
Fork	Tenedor
Spoon	Cuchara
Glass	Vaso
Cup	Taza

| Plate | Plato |

Ordering

English	Spanish
Hi, I'm—, and I'll be serving you	Hola, yo soy—y estaré sirviéndoles
What can I do for you?	¿Qué puedo hacer por ustedes?
Can I help you?	¿Puedo ayudarlo/a?
Can I take your coat?	¿Podría tomar su chaqueta?
Have you booked a table?	¿Ha reservado una mesa?
How many are you?	¿Cuántos son ustedes?
Follow me, please.	Sígame, por favor.
Can I take your order?	¿Puedo tomar su orden?
What would you like to start with?	¿Con qué le gustaría comenzar?
What would you like to drink?	¿Qué le gustaría para beber?
What would you like for dessert?	¿Qué le gustaría para el postre?
How would you like your steak?	¿Cómo le gustaría su carne?
Rare, medium, well done	Rojo inglés – crudo, medio, bien cocido

A table for two, please.	Una mesa para dos, por favor.
May we sit at this table?	¿Podríamos sentarnos en esta mesa?
The menu, please.	El menú, por favor.
What's on the menu?	¿Qué hay en el menú?
What's the specialty for today?	¿Cuál es la especialidad para hoy?
We are not ready yet.	Aún no estamos listos.
I'll have the lasagna, please.	Yo quiero lasaña, por favor.
Can you bring me a glass of water?	¿Podría traerme un vaso con agua?
I'll have the same	Yo quiero lo mismo.
That's all, thank you.	Eso es todo, gracias.
Can I have the bill, please?	¿Me podría traer la cuenta, por favor?
Here you are.	Aquí estás.
What can you recommend?	¿Qué nos puedes recomendar?
The rest is for you.	El resto es para ti.
Do you have wine by the glass?	¿Tiene vino por copa?

Please pay at the cash register. Por favor paguen en la caja registradora.

Today we have buffet for the breakfast. Hoy tenemos comida bufet para el desayuno.

Could I have chips instead of salad? ¿Podría traerme papas fritas en vez de ensalada?

Could you bring me a coffee, please? ¿Me traería un café, por favor?

I think you've made a mistake. Creo que ha cometido un error.

Would you like red wine or white wine? ¿Le gustaría vino rojo o vino blanco?

Do you still serve breakfast? ¿Aún sirven el desayuno?

Do you want a salad with it? ¿Quiere una ensalada con eso?

How much should we leave as a tip? ¿Qué tanto le deberíamos de dejar de propina al mesero?

I want a reservation for five people. Quisiera hacer una reservación para cinco personas.

Anything else? ¿Nada más?

The waiter is taking his time.	El camarero se está tardando mucho.
What kind of dressing?	¿Qué tipo de aderezo?
Anything to drink?	¿Algo para beber?
The French fries are very good.	Las patatas fritas están muy buenas.
Sorry, the carrots are off.	Perdón, las zanahorias se terminaron.
Is everything all right?	¿Está todo bien?
Did you enjoy your meal?	¿Les gustó su comida?
Are you paying together?	¿Pagarán juntos?
May I show you to a table?	¿Puedo conducirlo a una mesa?
There'll be a table free in a few minutes.	Habrá una mesa disponible en unos minutos.
It'll take about 20 minutes.	Tomará alrededor de veinte minutos.
Could you bring me an extra plate?	¿Podría traerme un plato extra?
Could I speak with the manager?	¿Podría hablar con el gerente?

Could you bring me the dessert menu?	¿Me podría traer el menú de postres?
This doesn't taste good.	Esto no tiene buen sabor.
Could you bring me a soda?	¿Me podría traer una soda?
This place is too expensive.	Este lugar es muy caro.
I would like to eat pizza	Me gustaría comer pizza
Do you mind if I have sushi?	¿Te importaría si pido sushi?
Have a good meal!	¡Buen provecho!

Here is a great YouTube video to help you with some of the pronunciations: https://www.youtube.com/watch?v=juHg1tgMmy4 [YouTube search: TOP 20 SPANISH FOOD WORDS]. I also recommend these videos: https://www.youtube.com/watch?v=rmyC9nL5Vf4 [YouTube search: Spanish for Restaurants (version 1)] and https://www.youtube.com/watch?v=-pYmgngNVDo [YouTube search: Learn Spanish Online - At the Restaurant].

Don't be shy – use your new Spanish language skills to order in restaurants. You'll find the staff will be patient and helpful, and you'll get better service, even for trying to order in Spanish. Also, many waiters and waitresses are keen to practice their English, so it could make for a fun night out as well as a valuable learning experience.

CHAPTER NINE

HOBBIES

Spanish people take their leisure time very seriously – they are some of the most laid back people in the world, and they love to party. Any conversation is likely to include something about hobbies and leisure activities, so it's a good topic to add to your Spanish agenda.

English	Spanish
Dance	Bailar
Sing	Cantar
Read	Leer
Play soccer	Jugar fútbol
Ice skating	Patinaje en hielo
Play video games	Jugar video juegos
Run	Correr
Swim	Nadar
Cook	Cocinar

Music   Música

CONVERSATIONS ABOUT HOBBIES

English	Spanish
Do you have a hobby?	¿Tienes algún pasatiempo?
Yes I do. I like dancing.	Sí tengo. Me gusta bailar.
Do you have a favorite hobby?	¿Tienes algún pasatiempo favorito?
I like to read	Me gusta leer
What kind of books do you like to read?	¿Qué tipo de libros te gusta leer?
I like reading biographies and romance.	Me gusta leer biografías y novelas románticas.
Do you like to dance?	¿Te gusta bailar?
What kind of dance do you like?	¿Qué tipo de baile te gusta?
I like dancing tango and salsa.	Me gusta bailar tango y salsa.
How about music?	¿Qué hay de la música?
What kind of music do you like?	¿Qué tipo de música te gusta escuchar?

I like listening to classical and jazz.	Me gusta escuchar música clásica y jazz.
Do you cook?	¿Tú cocinas?
I like cooking Greek and Spanish food.	Me gusta cocinar comida griega y española.
Have you ever run a 10k race?	¿Alguna vez has corrido diez kilómetros en una competencia?
How fast can you run 5k?	¿Cuánto tiempo te tomas en correr cinco kilómetros?
Do you like to cook as a hobby?	¿Te gusta cocinar como pasatiempo?
Have you ever been in a competition?	¿Alguna vez has estado en una competencia?
In my free time, I like to go to the club.	En mi tiempo libre me gusta ir a un club.
My friend won first place in dancing.	Mi amigo ganó el primer lugar en el baile.
Been to an international competition?	¿Has ido a una competencia internacional?

Where do you like to buy books? ¿Dónde te gusta comprar libros?

Knowing the vocabulary of leisure is a great way to initiate conversations in Spanish. It will also help you to understand more articles in Spanish newspapers, magazines and websites, even if you don't have any particular hobbies yourself.

CHAPTER TEN

EMERGENCIES

Unfortunately, life doesn't always go to plan, and you may experience an emergency, or be closely involved in one. You'll be able to cope better, and be more helpful as a bystander, if you have the vocabulary to deal with an emergency situation.

EMERGENCY SERVICES

Vocabulary

English	Spanish
Police	Policía
Fireman	Bomberos
Rescue Service	Servicio de Rescate
Military	Ejército
Mountain rescue	Rescate de montaña
Search and rescue	Búsqueda y rescate

English	Spanish
Forest fire suppression	Extinción de incendios forestales
Air search	Búsqueda aérea
Coast Guard	Guardia costera
Emergency management	Gestión de emergencias
Blood transplant supply	Suministro de transplante de sangre
Lifeboat	Bote salvavidas
Ambulances	Ambulancias
Fire extinguisher	Extintor de fuego
Emergency room	Urgencias
Fire tuck	Carro de bomberos
Burned	Quemado

Phrases

English	Spanish
Police!	¡Policía!
Help!	¡Ayuda!
Fire!	¡Fuego!
Call the fire brigade	Llama a los bomberos

Climb the ladder	Sube la escalera
We need a paramedic	Necesitamos un paramédico
Call 911	Llame al 911
Can you help me?	¿Me puede ayudar?
There's been an accident!	¡Ha habido un accidente!
Someone is injured	Hay un herido
Where is the police station?	¿Dónde está la estación de policía?
Someone has been run over	Atropellado a una persona
Someone has robbed me	Alguien me ha robado
I want to report a theft	Quiero denunciar un robo
I have been attacked	He sido agredido/a
My car has been stolen	Me han robado el carro/coche
I have been raped	He sido violado/a
I need to make an urgent phone call	Necesito hacer una llamada urgente
I did not know the speed limit	No sabía el límite de velocidad
How much is the fine?	¿De cuánto es la multa?
Do I have to pay it right away?	¿Tengo que pagarla inmediatamente?

I'm in danger	Estoy en peligro
This is an emergency	Ésta es una emergencia
There are screams at my neighbor's	Me gustaría reportar gritos en la casa de mi vecino
I think I heard a shot	Creo que escuché un disparo
Bring her to the hospital immediately	Tráela al hospital inmediatamente
Will he/she be safe?	¿Estará a salvo?
I need a blood donor!	¡Necesito un donador de sangre!
What is his blood type?	¿Qué tipo de sangre tiene él?
He has O+ blood	Él tiene sangre O+
There is too much smoke	Aquí hay mucho humo
I can't see anything	No puedo ver nada.
Is anyone else inside?	¿Hay alguien más adentro?

Here is a video that will give you a quick glimpse of how to pronounce these words in Spanish: https://www.youtube.com/watch?v=tI0nAKVaeZ8 [YouTube search: How to Speak Spanish : Knowing Common Spanish Phrases for Emergencies].

MEDICAL HELP

The first thing you probably need to learn how to say is that you need help. The Spanish phrase for —I need help‖ is —*necesito ayuda*‖. Here is a video on how to say just that: https://www.youtube.com/watch?v=NtkveRgwd2s [YouTube search: How to Say "I Need Help" in Spanish]. After saying this, you can use any of the other words here to pass your message across. When you combine that with what you learn in the phrases section, I'm sure you will get all the help you need.

Vocabulary

English	Spanish
Wound	La herida
Weak	Débil
Twisted	Torcido
To vomit	Vomitar
To sneeze	Estornudar
To shake	Temblar
To injure	Herir
To have a cold	Estar resfriado
To faint	Desmayar

To cough	Toser
To break	Romper
To bleed	Sangrar
To be sick	Vomitar
To be burned	Estar incendiado
Tired	Cansado
Tablet	El comprimido
Syrup	El jarabe
Symptom	El síntoma
Swollen	Hinchado
Surgeon	El/la cirujano
Sunstroke	La insolación
Stomach ache	El dolor del estómago
Stinging	El escozor
Sprain	Una torcedura/ el esguince
Sore throat	El dolor de la garganta

Sickness, illness	La enfermedad
Sick	Enfermo
Sea sickness	El mareo
Rash	El sarpullido
Private hospital	El hospital privado
Prescription	La prescripción /la receta /el récipe
Plaster	El emplasto /el yeso
Pill	La pastilla
Physical	El examen médico
Patient	La/el paciente
Paracetamol	El paracetamol
Pain	El dolor
Operation	La operación
Ointment, cream	La pomada
Nurse	La enfermera/ el enfermero
Nausea	El mareo /Náuseas

Migraine	Migraña
Medicine	El medicamento/ la medicina
Medication	La medicación
Irritation	El picor
Injury	Herida
Injection /shot	La inyección
Inhaler	El inhalador
Inflammation	La inflamación
Hospital	El hospital
Heart attack	Un/El ataque cardíaco
Health	La salud
Headache	El dolor de cabeza
Fracture	La fractura
Flu	La gripe
Fever	La fiebre
Eyedrops	El colirio
Emergency room	La sala de emergencia

Dressing	El vendaje
Doctor's consulting room	El consultorio
Doctor	El doctor/ el médico
Dizzy	Mareado
Diarrhea	La diarrea
Dead	Muerto/a
Cut	El corte
Cramp	El calambre
Cough	La tos
Cold	La gripe/ el resfriado / resfriado
Clinic	La clínica
Broken bone	Fractura
Broken	Roto
Break	La rotura
Blood	La sangre
Aspirin	La aspirina
Anti-inflammatory	El antiinflamatorio

Antihistamine	El antihistamínico
Antibiotic	El antibiótico
Allergy	La alergia
Allergic	Alérgico
Air sickness	El mareo en el avión (Mal de aviadores)
Accident	El accidente
Throat	Garganta
The wrists	Las muñecas
The womb, uterus	El útero
The womb	La matriz
The veins	Las venas
The vagina	La vagina
The torso, body	El tronco
The tongue	La lengua
The thighs	Los muslos
The teeth	Los dientes

The stomach	El estómago
The spine	La columna vertebral
The small intestine	El intestino delgado
The skin	La piel
The penis	El pene
The pancreas	El páncreas
The ovaries	Los ovarios
The esophagus	El esófago
The nose	La nariz
The neck	El cuello
The muscles	Los músculos
The mouth	La boca
The liver	El hígado
The lips	Los labios
The legs	Las piernas
The large intestine	El intestino grueso

The knees	Las rodillas
The kidneys	Los riñones
The intestines	Los intestinos
The heels	Los talones
The head	La cabeza
The hands	Las manos
The hair	El cabello
The hair	El pelo
The glands	Las glándulas
The gallbladder	La vesícula biliar
The forehead	La frente
The fingers	Los dedos
The feet	Los pies
The face	La cara
The eyes	Los ojos
The ears	Las orejas
The colon	El colon

The chin	El mentón
The cheeks	Los cachetes, las mejillas
The calves	Las pantorrillas
The buttocks	Las nalgas
The brain	El cerebro
The bones	Los huesos
The blood	La sangre
The bladder	La vejiga
The back	La espalda
The appendix	El apéndice
Nails	Uñas
Back of the neck	La nuca
Back	Espalda
Arms	Brazos
Abdomen	Abdomen
Chemist	Farmacéutico

This YouTube video should help you say whatever you want to say in a better way: https://www.youtube.com/watch?v=kQm_6ZKKyGA [YouTube search: Learn Spanish! - Parts of the body]. Another great video is https://www.youtube.com/watch?v=dTrFeTDdXqU [YouTube search: Las Partes Del Cuerpo Para Niños, Our Body Parts In Spanish For Children (Video Infantil)].

Phrases

English	Spanish
Call an ambulance	Llama una ambulancia
You need to recover	Necesitas recuperarte
Where is the pharmacy?	¿Dónde está la farmacia?
Where is the hospital?	¿Dónde está el hospital?
My stomach hurts	Me duele el estómago
My nails need to be cut	Mis uñas tienen que cortarse
My leg hurts	Me duele la pierna
My injury is getting worst	Mi herida se está poniendo peor
My head hurts.	Me duele la cabeza.
My eyes hurt	Me duelen los ojos
My eyes are dry	Mis ojos están secos

My blood type is—	Mi tipo de sangre es—
My back hurts	Me duele la espalda
My arm hurts	Me duele el brazo
Maybe you need glasses	Tal vez necesitas anteojos
I've broken my—	Me he roto—
It is not serious.	No es de gravedad.
I'm having trouble breathing	Tengo problemas al respirar
I'd like to go to the hospital	Quiero ir al hospital
I'm feeling dizzy	Me siento mareado
I'm allergic to nuts	Soy alérgico a las nueces.
I think I've broken my leg.	Creo que me he roto la pierna
I take— (the name of medicine)	Yo tomo— (the name of medicine)
I need to go to the hospital	Necesito ir al hospital.
I need to buy tablets	Necesito comprar tabletas
I need this medicine	Necesito esta medicina
I need something for the flu	Necesito algo para la gripe
I need a doctor	Necesito un doctor

I have a stomachache.	Me duele el estomago.
I have high blood pressure	Tengo presión alta
I have heart problems	Tengo problemas cardíacos
I have diarrhea	Tengo diarrea
I have cut myself	Me he cortado
I have been vomiting	Tengo vómito
I have asthma	Tengo asma
I have an allergy to penicillin.	Tengo alergia a la penicilina.
I have a toothache	Tengo dolor en un diente
I have a temperature.	Tengo fiebre.
I have a pain here	Tengo un dolor aquí
I have a fever	Tengo fiebre
I have a cold	Estoy resfriado
I had a heart attack	Tuve un ataque al corazón
I feel sick	Me siento enfermo
I don't feel so well	No me siento muy bien

I am sick	Estoy enfermo/a
I am having chest pain	Tengo dolor en el pecho
I am feeling bad	Me siento mal
I am diabetic	Soy diabético/soy diabética
I am allergic to—	Soy alérgico/a—
How do you feel?	¿Cómo te sientes?
He has fever	Él tiene fiebre
Do you have something for ...?	¿Tiene algo para ...?
Do you have insurance?	¿Tienes seguro?
Could you call the doctor?	¿Podría llamar al doctor?
Can you give me a painkiller?	¿Puede darme algo para el dolor?

TOILETRIES

Vocabulary

English	Spanish
Mirror	Espejo
Toothpaste	Pasta dental
Toothbrush	Cepillo de dientes

English	Spanish
Dental floss	Hilo dental
Hair brush	Cepillo de pelo
Bathtub	Bañera
Nails	Uñas
Nail polish	Pintura de uñas

Phrases

English	Spanish
Brush your teeth after every meal.	Después de cada comida, lávate los dientes.
I couldn't brush my hair today.	No pude cepillar mi cabello el día de hoy.
Before going to bed, floss your teeth	Antes de ir a la cama, usa el hilo dental.
I couldn't do my nails today.	No pude hacerme mis uñas el día de hoy.
Is there toothpaste in your bathroom?	¿Tienes pasta dental en tu baño?
I don't have toothpaste.	No tengo pasta dental.

I need to buy a new toothbrush.	Necesito comprar un nuevo cepillo de dientes.
My nails are too long.	Mis uñas están muy largas.

Try pronouncing the words and phrases above; then search them on YouTube to confirm whether you got them right.

The vocabulary in this chapter will help you if you are involved in an emergency situation, or if you are ill and cannot find an English speaking health professional. If nothing else, learn the standard phrases for summoning help, and the names of the most common body parts and ailments. Life isn't always a beach – even in Spain!

CHAPTER ELEVEN

AT THE HOTEL

If you need to spend the night in a hotel where people speak Spanish, this section will help you greatly. For starters, here are a few Spanish words to use for common items that you will find in a hotel, and some phrases to try out. Later, there will be links to a few YouTube videos that you can watch to help you with your pronunciation and accent.

VOCABULARY

English	Spanish
Bathroom	Baño
Toilet paper	Papel de baño
Soap	Jabón
Shampoo	Champú
Bed	Cama
Towel	Toalla

Double room	Cuarto doble
Elevator	Ascensor
Key	Llave
Blanket	Cobija
Pillow	Almohada
Television	Televisión
Lobby	Entrada
Manager	El/la gerente
Room service	Servicio de cuarto
Shower	Ducha
Porter	El portero
Bellhop	Botones
Guest	Huésped
Balcony	Balcón
Air-conditioner	Aire acondicionado
Bathtub	Bañera
Bill	Cuenta

Receipt	Recibo
Breakfast	Desayuno
Lunch	Almuerzo
Dinner	Cena
Double bed	Cama matrimonial
Full board	Pensión completa
Half board	Media pensión
Boarding house	Pensión
Pool	Piscina

PHRASES

English	Spanish
Can you suggest a cheap hotel?	¿Puede recomendarme un hotel barato?
What's the price per night?	¿Cuál es el precio por noche?
I would like a single room.	Me gustaría un cuarto sencillo.
May I see the room?	¿Podría ver el cuarto?
There isn't any hot water.	No hay agua caliente.
Where is our room?	¿Dónde está nuestra habitación?

Could you bring us more toilet paper? ¿Nos traería más papel de baño?

I don't like this room.	No me gusta esta habitación.
What's the weekly rate?	¿Cuánto cuesta por semana?
Are meals included?	¿Están incluidas las comidas?
My room number is—	El número de mi habitación es—

The television doesn't work. La televisión no funciona.

One of the lights isn't working. Una de las luces no está funcionando.

Could you please call me a taxi? ¿Podría por favor llamar a un taxi?

After midnight you need to ring the bell. Después de media noche, necesitará tocar el timbre.

I'll be back around ten o'clock. Estaré de regreso alrededor de las diez en punto.

What time do I need to check out? ¿A qué hora necesito entregar la habitación?

Could I have an extra blanket?	¿Me podría dar una cobija extra?
Could I have a towel, please?	¿Me podría dar una toalla, por favor?
My room has not been made up.	Aún no se ha limpiado mi habitación.
I have lost my room key.	He perdido la llave de mi habitación.
The key doesn't work.	La llave no funciona.
There isn't any hot water.	No hay agua caliente.
The room behind me is too noisy.	La habitación de al lado es muy ruidosa.
Do not disturb.	No molestar.
Please make up the room.	Por favor limpiar la habitación.
Is there a pool?	¿Hay alguna piscina?
Do you have gym?	¿Tienen gimnasio?
The pool will be open until 9:00 pm.	La piscine estará abierta hasta las nueve de la noche.

Could you wake me up at 7:00 am? ¿Me podría levantar a las siete en punto de la mañana?

Nice view.   Bonita vista.

This pillow is uncomfortable.   Esta almohada es incómoda.

How long are you staying?   ¿Cuánto tiempo se van a quedar?

I can't fall asleep.   No puedo conciliar el sueño.

Do you have a living room?   ¿Tienen sala de estar?

Do you have room service?   ¿Tienen servicio a la habitación?

Where is the remote control?   ¿Dónde está el control remoto?

Excuse me, do you have ice?   Disculpe, tienen hielo?

I have three YouTube videos that will enhance your pronunciation greatly, each of them with a unique approach:

- https://www.youtube.com/watch?v=7g8faJxcC5Y

    o [YouTube search: Spanish Lessons # 3 - 15 Basic Spanish Sentences that you need to speak in a hotel]

- https://www.youtube.com/watch?v=LRJWdGDTCI8

- o [YouTube search: How to Speak Spanish : Common Spanish Phrases for Hotels]
- https://www.youtube.com/watch?v=slIfcKD-pXY
  - o [YouTube search: how 2 learn spanish : at the hotel]

Those who work in the hospitality trade appreciate it when people try to speak Spanish, and you will often find you get better service. Also, bar and hotel staff can be great sources of extra tuition, since they will correct your mistakes in return for being able to practice their English on you. It all adds to the Spanish learning experience!

CHAPTER TWELVE

SHOPPING

This section should help make your shopping a lot easier in a Spanish speaking territory. Shopping in Spain is fun – and it's even more fun when you can ask for what you want in Spanish.

On a cultural note, don't be in too much of a hurry to get what you want. Spanish people will chat to each other, either in person or on the phone, either while they're serving you or instead of serving you. It's nothing personal, and it's not because you're a foreigner – it's just the way it is!

The word *tienda* means ‚store,' but in Spain, stores often take the suffix ‚ería' with the service they offer to make up their name. So for example, a hairdresser's is a *peluquería*, a baker's is a *panadería*, and a book store is a *librería*. These derive from the nouns *peluquero/a, pan* and *libro*, meaning hairdresser, bread and book. Store names always take the feminine gender.

VOCABULARY

English	Spanish
Basket	Cesta/Canasta
Shopping cart	Carrito de compras
Newsstand	Quiosco
Clothes shop	Tienda de modas
Marketplace	Plaza de mercado
To go shopping	Ir de compras
Buy	Comprar
Pay	Pagar
Open	Abierto
Cheap	Barato
Expensive	Caro
Closed	Cerrado
Closed for lunch	Cerrado por almuerzo
Credit card	Tarjeta de crédito
Jewelers	Joyería, Joyeros

English	Spanish
Shoe store	Zapatería
Exit	Salida
Entrance	Entrada
Better quality	Mejor calidad
Receipt	Recibo
Defective	Defectuoso
Broken	Roto
Change	Cambiar
Return	Devolver
Dress	Vestido
Blouse	Blusa
Skirt	Falda
Belt	Cinturón
Shoes	Zapatos
Stockings	Medias
Underwear	Ropa interior
Jeans	Pantalones

Shorts	Pantalonetas
Handbag	Bolso
Sandals	Sandalias
Tight	Apretado
Match	Combinar

PHRASES

English	Spanish
How much is this?	¿Cuánto cuesta esto?
It's too expensive.	Es demasiado caro.
Do you have anything cheaper?	¿Tiene algo más barato?
Can I try it on?	¿Puedo probármelo?
I don't like this color.	No me gusta este color.
Where are the changing rooms?	¿Dónde están los probadores?
I'm going to pay cash.	Voy a pagar con efectivo.
Can you help me?	¿Puede atenderme?
Do you have another size?	¿Tiene otra talla?
I'm just looking, thank you.	Solo estoy mirando, gracias.
Could you show me that dress?	¿Podría mostrarme ese vestido?

English	Spanish
Excuse me, this is broken.	Disculpe, esto está roto.
Where can I buy—?	¿Dónde puedo comprar—?
They are very pretty.	Son muy bonitos/bonitas.
Where is the cash register?	¿Dónde está la caja registradora?
Does this have a discount?	¿Esto tiene descuento?
This is on sale.	Esto está en oferta.
I'll come back later.	Regresaré más tarde.
This doesn't fit. Can I get a bigger one?	Esto no me queda. ¿Me podría traer uno más grande?
I don't care for any of this.	No me gusta nada de esto.
How much do you charge for this?	¿Cuánto cobran por esto?
Please, can you wrap it up?	Por favor, ¿puede envolverlo?
Ask the saleswomen/man	Pregúntele a la venderora/vendedor
Take the elevator	Tome el elevador
Where is the men's department?	¿Dónde está el departamento de ropa de hombres?

Do you have change for a twenty? ¿Tiene cambio para veinte dólares?

The colors don't match.   Los colores no coinciden.

The skirt is too short.   La falda es muy corta.

The dress is too long. I won't wear it. El vestido es muy largo. No lo usaré.

Let me get you a shorter one.   Déjeme traerle uno más corto.

Excuse me, do you have another size? Disculpe, ¿tiene otra talla?

Where is the underwear section? ¿Dónde está la sección de ropa interior?

To help you master your pronunciation, here are three YouTube videos to help you:

- https://www.youtube.com/watch?v=IXL4sr3T0cg
    - [YouTube search: Spanish 101 Shopping Level One]
- https://www.youtube.com/watch?v=YlsDjxLY7vk
    - [YouTube search: How to Speak Spanish - Learn to shop in Spanish]

- https://www.youtube.com/watch?v=wfi8lT0P6jk
    - [YouTube search: How to Speak Spanish : Common Spanish Phrases for Shopping]

Remember that when asking questions – and you'll be asking a lot of questions when you go shopping – it's the inflection in your voice, rather than just the vocabulary, that conveys the question. If you're shopping at the market, you're expected to haggle, unless you're buying produce, in which case you pay the going rate. Going shopping is an excellent way to practice your Spanish and learn new vocabulary, so make the most of this pleasant learning opportunity whenever you can.

CHAPTER THIRTEEN

POST OFFICE AND MOVIES

In this chapter, I won't provide links to YouTube videos for practice; you will do that. Try practicing the words and phrases first, and then search for relevant videos to see if you have gotten them right. If you have followed the guide and visited the videos, you should now have a better accent even if you are a beginner.

POST OFFICE

If you want to send snail mail when you are in a country where Spanish is the dominant language, knowing what to say will ensure a much easier time with the staff. Keep in mind many postal workers won't understand English so you'll have to speak Spanish to them. The Post Office – or Oficina de Correo Postal, Correos – is similar to shops and stores in that the workers are not averse to chatting to other customers or on the phone while they serve you. Even a business call will entail enquiries after family members before they get to the heart of the matter, so expect to wait around!

Vocabulary

English	Spanish
Stamp	Estampilla
Envelope	Sobre
Mailbox	Buzón
Adress	Dirección
Return address	Remitente
Letter carrier	Cartero
Mail	Correo
Letter	Carta
Postcard	Tarjeta postal
Pen	Bolígrafo, Lapicero

Phrases

English	Spanish
Is there a post office nearby?	¿Hay alguna oficina postal cerca de aquí?
Is there any mail for me?	¿Hay correspondencia para mí?
At what time does it open?	¿A qué horas abren?

I want some stamps for this letter. Quiero algunas estampillas para esta carta.

I want to send it via air-mail, please. Quiero enviarlo por correo aéreo, por favor.

Can I send a money order from here? ¿Puedo enviar un giro postal desde aquí?

Could you weigh this letter for me? ¿Podría pesar ésta carta?

I would like to register this letter. Me gustaría registrar esta carta.

Where is the mailbox? ¿Dónde está el buzón?

How long would it take to get to Spain? ¿Cuánto se tardaría en llegar a España?

I don't know the zip code of this city. No sé el código postal de este país.

How can I send this faster? ¿Cómo puedo enviar esto más rápido?

Could I send this box? ¿Podría mandar esta caja?

Let me check the address Déjeme chequear la dirección.

How much would it be? ¿Cuánto me costaría?
Where can I buy envelopes? ¿Dónde puedo comprar sobres?

Could you help me fill out this form? ¿Me podría ayudar a llenar este formulario?

Excuse me, do you have cards? Disculpe, ¿tiene tarjetas?

What kind of cards do you have? ¿Qué tipos de tarjetas tienen?

Do you sell thank-you cards? ¿Venden tarjetas de agradecimiento?

Could you lend me a pen, please? Me podría prestar un bolígrafo, por favor?

MOVIE THEATER

If you are going out for a movie, knowing what different words mean and how to pronounce them will definitely be a plus. And watching a movie in Spanish will help with your pronunciation. Try watching a movie you're familiar with in English that's been dubbed in Spanish to help you improve your vocabulary. If you're having fun while you're learning, it will sink in better.

Vocabulary

English	Spanish
Film	Película
Premiere	Estreno
Genre	Género

English	Spanish
Comedy	Comedia
Horror film	Película de terror
Action film	Película de acción
Science fiction	Ciencia ficción
Drama film	Película de drama
Soda	Soda
Room	Sala
Animation	Animación
Scriptwriter	Guionista
Director	Director
Drama	Drama
Ticket office	Taquilla
Seat	Butaca
Usher	Acomodador
Allocated seating	Entrada numerada
Matinée	Sesión matinal
Discount day	Día de descuento

Popcorn	Poporopos, Palomitas de maíz, Rosetas de maíz
Soft drink	Refresco
Chocolate bar	Barra de chocolate

Phrases

English	Spanish
Let's go to the movies!	¡Vamos al cine!
What's on at the movies today?	¿Qué hay en el cine hoy?
At what time does the film start?	¿A qué hora comienza la película?
How long does it last?	¿Cuánto tiempo dura?
What kind of film is it?	¿Qué clase de película es esa?
It's a horror movie.	Es una película de terror.
What's it about?	¿De qué se trata?
I liked the actors' performance.	Me gusto la actuación de los actores.
Where is the movie room?	¿Dónde está la sala de la película?
I want to buy some popcorn.	Quiero comprar unos poporopos (unas palomitas de maíz).

Can I get an entertainment guide? ¿Puedo adquirir una guía de entretenimiento?

I want two tickets, please. Quiero dos boletos, por favor.

What movie theater will the film be in? ¿En qué cine será la película?

Is it subtitled? ¿Está subtitulada?

At what time does it start? ¿A qué hora comienza?

How was the movie? ¿Cómo estuvo la película?

It was boring. Estuvo aburrida.
I would prefer to see a romantic movie. Preferiría ver una película romántica

When is the premiere of the movie? ¿Cuándo sera el estreno de la película?

It will be on September 5th. Será el cinco de septiembre.

Have you ever met an actor? ¿Alguna vez has conocido a un actor?

The movie was so sad. La película estuvo triste.

I liked the movie. Me gustó la película.

I like independent movies. Me gusta el cine independiente.

This is a nice movie theatre.　　　　Este es un bonito cine.

When is the next showing?　¿Cuándo es la próxima función?

We should go to the movies more often. Deberíamos venir al cine más seguido.

Now you should be armed with all the phrases you need to have a great night at the movies. Enjoy!

CHAPTER FOURTEEN

FEELINGS AND EMOTIONS

The Spanish are a very vocal and emotional race, so they're going to be telling you how they feel, as well as asking about your state of mind. Remember that emotions are a temporary state, so if you are sad, you would use the verb *estar* rather than *ser*. So you would say *estoy triste*, rather than *soy triste*.

VOCABULARY
English　　　　　**Spanish**

English	Spanish
Angry	Enojado/a
Agitated	Agitado/a
Anxious	Ansioso/a
Ashamed	Avergonzado/a
Bored	Aburrido/a
Confused	Confundido/a
Depressed	Deprimido/a
Excited	Emocionado/a
Frightened	Aterrado/a
Frustrated	Frustrado/a
Furious	Furioso/a
Guilty	Culpable
Happy	Feliz
Jealous	Celoso/a
Proud	Orgulloso/a
Sad	Triste
Shy	Tímido/a

Sleepy	Somnoliento/a
Surprised	Sorprendido/a
Thankful	Agradecido/a
Worried	Preocupado/a
Lucky	Afortunado/a

This YouTube video should help you in pronouncing some of the words above: https://www.youtube.com/watch?v=ortoiFYj6nw [YouTube search: Expressing Feelings in Spanish : Expresar Sentimientos en Español]. Another helpful video is at https://www.youtube.com/watch?v=3F5WNHt0Fso [YouTube search: Learn Spanish! - Describing feelings with Estar (to be)].

PHRASES

English	Spanish
Today I feel happy.	Hoy me siento feliz.
I feel guilty for him.	Me siento culpable por él.
He is a shy person.	Él es una persona tímida.
Today I felt lucky.	Hoy me sentí afortunado.
I feel excited about tomorrow's trip.	Me siento emocionado por el viaje de mañana.

I'm sick. I can't go to the party.	Estoy enfermo. No puedo ir a la fiesta.
I feel confused.	Me siento confundida.
How do you feel today?	¿Cómo te sientes hoy?
I was bored watching a movie.	Estaba aburrido mientras miraba una película.
I feel betrayed.	Me siento traicionada.
Jerry said he was feeling sad today.	Jerry dijo que se sentía un poco deprimido el día de hoy.
Some have luck, some not.	Algunos tienen suerte, otros no.

These words and phrases should help you to discuss your own emotions and adopt the appropriate tone when other people answer fully and honestly when you say _How are you today?'

CHAPTER FIFTEEN

LOVE AND RELATIONSHIPS

Following on naturally from emotions, this chapter will help you pronounce words properly when talking about love, relationships, weddings etc. I won't provide videos for this chapter either. Considering how far you have come, you should be able to pronounce these words if you have been following the lessons keenly.

VOCABULARY

English	Spanish
Love	Amor
In love	Enamorado/a
Break up	Terminar
Engaged	Comprometidos
Fiancée	Prometida
Relationship	Relación

English	Spanish
Dating	Cita
Girlfriend	Novia
Boyfriend	Novio
Bridal veil	Velo de novia
To cuddle/hug	Abrazar (Un abrazo is a hug)
Cheat	Engañar
Fidelity	Fidelidad
Beautiful	Hermosa
Handsome	Guapo
Pretty	Bonita
Argue	Discutir
Flirt	Coquetear
Kiss	Beso
Attract	Atraer

PHRASES

English	Spanish
I feel attracted to you.	Me siento atraído/a por ti/usted.
Can I kiss you?	¿Te puedo besar?

English	Spanish
I'm falling in love with you.	Me estoy enamorando de ti
Do you want to be my girlfriend?	¿Quieres ser mi novia?
She is my fiancée.	Ella es mi prometida.
Give me a hug.	Dame un abrazo.
My boyfriend cheated on me.	Mi novio me engañó.
My boyfriend and I argued.	Mi novio y yo discutimos.
She is flirting with me.	Ella está coqueteando conmigo.
I just invited my family and best friends.	Solo invité a mi familia y mis mejores amigos.
I like to cuddle you.	Me gusta abrazarte.
We got a lot of wedding presents.	Recibimos muchos regalos de boda.
I declare you husband and wife.	Los declare marido y mujer.
My friend is dating someone.	Mi amiga está saliendo con alguien.
Where is my bridal veil?	¿Dónde está mi velo de novia?
Who is the bride?	¿Quién es la novia?
Who are the godparents?	¿Quiénes son los padrinos?

Are you sure you want to get married?	¿Estás segura que te quieres casar?
Is he handsome?	¿Es guapo?
Our religious wedding is at—church.	Tendremos nuestra boda religiosa en la iglesia—.
He broke up with me.	Él rompió conmigo.
You are beautiful.	Eres hermosa.
I love you.	Te amo.
Would you go on a date with me?	¿Irías a una cita conmigo?
Are you engaged?	¿Están comprometidos?
We are in a relationship.	Estamos en una relación.
Do you want to marry me?	¿Te quieres casar conmigo?
We are engaged.	Estamos comprometidos.

AT A WEDDING

Once love progresses to the wedding, there's some more vocabulary to learn. Confusingly, *la novia* refers to the bride, as well as the girlfriend. However, in context it's not so hard to understand. If you're fortunate enough to be invited to a Spanish *boda* (wedding), prepare to have a great time, and don't forget to practice your Spanish as much as possible.

Vocabulary

English	Spanish
Wedding dress	Vestido de novia
Wedding ring	Anillo de bodas
Bridesmaid	Dama de honor
Bride	Novia
Invitations	Invitaciones
Top hat	Sombrero de copa
Church	Iglesia
Suit	Traje
Bouquet	Ramo
Toast	Brindis
Wedding party	Fiesta de bodas
Witness	Testigo
Wedding cake	Pastel de bodas
Wedding planner	Planificador de bodas
Honeymoon	Luna de miel
Guests	Invitados

English	Spanish
Husband	Marido
Wife	Esposa
Waltz	Vals

Phrases

English	Spanish
They got married.	Ellos se casaron.
The bride threw the bouquet.	La novia tiró el buqué.
The guests were happy.	Los invitados estaban felices.
The wedding dress is ready.	El vestido de la novia está listo.
Everyone was excited for the wedding.	Todos estaban emocionados por la boda.
Congratulations to the married couple.	Felicidades a la pareja de casados.
Can I put the wedding ring on you?	¿Puedo ponerte el anillo de bodas?
Where will you spend your honeymoon?	¿Dónde van a pasar su luna de miel?
The wedding cake was delicious.	El pastel de bodas estaba delicioso.

The newlyweds went on a honeymoon. La pareja de casados fue a su luna de miel.

The bridesmaids all wore red dresses. Todas las damas de honor estaban vestidas con un vestido rojo.

Will you be my wife? ¿Aceptas ser mi esposa?

Will you be my husband? ¿Aceptas ser mi esposo?

It's time for the couple to dance a waltz. Es hora de que la pareja baile el vals.

The wedding planner organized it all. La planificadora de bodas organizó cada detalle.

It's time for the toast. Es hora del brindis.

The couple will honeymoon in Hawaii. La pareja de casados irá a Hawai para su luna de miel.

How do you feel now you're married? ¿Cómo se sienten ahora que están casados?

We feel more in love than ever. Sentimos que nos amamos más que nunca.

How long is your honeymoon? ¿Cuánto tiempo estarán de luna de miel?

While the vocabulary for weddings is somewhat specialized, learning it will help you to fit in with your Spanish friends and neighbors. Everyone loves a wedding, and you'll have a great time if you can chat to the guests in their own language.

CHAPTER SIXTEEN

JOBS

In this chapter, I will give you important phrases that you can use when talking about work, careers, and jobs. Just like in the previous chapter, try to pronounce the words and then look up the correct pronunciations. If you're intending to be in Spain for any length of time, and you need to earn your keep, this chapter will give you a head start in the Spanish workplace.

VOCABULARY

Professions

English	Spanish
Cook	Cocinero

English	Spanish
Customs officer	Aduanero
Artist	Artista
Actor	Actor
Actress	Actriz
Doctor	Doctor/Médico
Driver	Chófer
Editor	Editor/a
Housewife	Ama de casa
Lawyer	Abogado
Musician	Músico
Writer	Escritor
Teacher	Maestro
Designer	Diseñador
Seller	Vendedor

Applying for a job

English	Spanish
Interview	Entrevista
Earn	Ganar
Hired	Contratado
Fired	Despedido
Experience	Experiencia
Business	Negocios
Call center	Centro de llamadas
Work	Trabajo
Schedule	Horario
Office	Oficina
Paper	Papel
Marker	Marcador
Stapler	Engrapadora

PHRASES

English	Spanish
At what time is the interview?	¿A qué hora es la entrevista?

How should I dress for the interview? ¿Cómo me debería vestir para la entrevista?

Do you have experience? ¿Tienes experiencia?

How long have you worked in sales? ¿Por cuánto tiempo has trabajado como vendedor?

How much do you expect to earn? ¿Cuánto esperas ganar?

What kind of schedule do you want? ¿Qué tipo de horario estás buscando?

Why do you want this job? ¿Por qué quieres este trabajo?

Why do you want to work here? ¿Por qué quieres trabajar aquí?

Do you want full time or part time? ¿Quieres tiempo completo o medio tiempo?

What do you know how to do? ¿Qué sabes hacer?

When can you start? ¿Cuándo puedes empezar?

Do you want a salary or a wage? ¿Quiéres ser pagado por mes o por hora?

You are hired. Estás contratado.

You are fired.	Estás despedido.
Tell me about yourself.	Hábleme de usted.
What are your strengths?	¿Cuáles son sus fortalezas?
What are your weaknesses?	¿Cuáles son sus debilidades?
What's your profession?	¿Cuál es tu profesión?

If you're from Northern Europe or North America, you should be aware that Spanish wages and salaries are much lower than you may be accustomed to. Another consideration is the siesta – many Spanish businesses and services close for two or three hours from around 2.00 pm and then resume trading later, so although you may work the same number of hours as previously, the actual working day is longer.

CHAPTER SEVENTEEN

SPORTS

Spanish speakers love sports. Whether it is football (soccer), volleyball, polo, tennis etc., you will find Spanish speakers at the top levels of play. As such, you might want to know a few words that describe different sports in Spanish just to ensure that you don't end up clueless when people are talking about the latest results.

VOCABULARY

English	Spanish
Wrestling	La lucha libre, la lucha grecorromana
Windsurfing	El windsurfing
Whitewater rafting	El rafting en aguas bravas
Waterskiing	El esquí náutico, el esquí acuático
Water polo	El polo acuático
Walking	La caminata

Wakeboarding	El wakeboarding
Volleyball	El voleibol
Triathlon	El triatlón
Track & field	El campo y pista, el atletismo
The team	El equipo
The game	El partido
Tennis	El tenis
Team handball	Balonmano
Team	El equipo
Table tennis	El tenis de mesa
Swimming	La natación
Surfing	El surfing
Squash	El squash
Sportsman	El/la deportista
Sport	El deporte
Softball	El sofbol
Soccer	El fútbol , el futbol
Snow skiing	El esquiar

Snowshoeing	El snowshoeing
Snowboarding	El snowboarding
Snorkeling	El snorkeling, el buzo superficial
Skydiving	El paracaidismo, el salto a paracaídas
Skis	Unos esquís
Skiing	El esquí
Ski poles	Unos bastones
Skating	El patinaje
Skateboarding	El skateboarding
Sharpshooting	El tiro al blanco
Scuba diving	El buceo
Sandboarding	El sandboarding
Sailing	El deporte de vela
Running	El correr
Rugby	El rugby
Rowing	El remo
Rodeo	El rodeo

Rock climbing	El alpinismo
Riding	La equitación
Repelling	El descenso de barrancos
Racquetball	El racquetball
Racket	Una raqueta
Pool	La piscina
Polo	El polo
Pole vault	El salto con pértiga
Player	El jugador
Ping-Pong	El tenis de mesa
Petanque	La petanca
Paragliding	El vuelo libre, el parapente
Paintball	El paintball
Olympics	Los Juegos Olímpicos, Las Olimpiadas
Net	Una red
Mountain climbing	El alpinismo
Motorcycle racing	El motociclismo

English	Spanish
Modern pentathlon	El pentatlón
Match	El partido
Martial arts	Los artes marciales
Marathon	El maratón
Long jump	El salto de longitud
Lacrosse	El lacrosse
Korfball	El korfbol
Kick boxing	El kick boxing
Kayaking	El piragüismo
Karate	El kárate
Jogging	El correr
Javelin throw	El lanzamiento de jabalina
Jai alai	El jai alai, el frontenis
Ice hockey	El hockey sobre hielo
Hunting	La caza
Horseback riding	La equitación
Horse racing	La carrera de caballos

Hockey	El jockey
Hiking	La caminata
High jump	El salto de altura
Helmet	El casco
Hang gliding	El vuelo libre, el vuelo con ala delta
Handball	El balonmano
Gymnastics	La gimnástica, la gimnasia
Golf	El golf
Glove	Un guante
Game	El juego
Frisbee	El disco volante
Soccer /football	El fútbol
Fishing	La pesca
Fencing	La esgrima
Exercise	El entrenamiento, los ejercicios
Draw	El empate

Discus throw	El lanzamiento de disco
Darts	El juego de flechillas
Cycling	El ciclismo
Cup	La copa
Croquet	El croquet
Cricket	El criquet
Cleats	Unos zapatos de fútbol
Chess	El ajedrez
Championship	El campeonato
Canoeing	El canotaje
Camping	El acampar, campamento
Bungee jumping	El saltar del amortiguador auxiliar, salto por cuerda elástica
Bullfight	La corrida de toros
Boxing	El boxeo
Bowling	El juego de bolos, el deporte de bochas
Boots	Unas botas

Bodybuilding	La halterofilia
Bocce	El deporte de bochas
Bobsledding	El paseo en trineo
Boating	El paseo en lancha, el paseo en bote
Billiards	El billar
Biking	El ciclismo
Bat	Un bate
Basketball hoop	Una canasta
Basketball	El básquetbol / el baloncesto
Baseball	El beisbol, el béisbol
Ball	La pelota/ un balón
Badminton	El badminton, el juego de raqueta y volante
Backpacking	La caminata con mochila
Auto racing	El rally, el automovilismo
Athletics	El atletismo
Archery	El tiro con arco
A football ground	Un campo de fútbol

A cricket pitch	Un terreno de criquet
A ski slope, piste	Una pista (de esquí)
A stadium	Un estadio
Applause	El aplauso
Coach	El director técnico
Defender	El defensa
First half	El primer tiempo
Forward	El delantero
Goalkeeper	El portero
Half time	El entretiempo
Ice rink	Una pista de hielo
Injury	La lesión
Linesman	El juez de línea
Loser	El perdedor
Midfielder	El centrocampista
Penalty	El penalti

English	Spanish
Qualifier	La eliminatoria
Red card	La tarjeta roja
Second half	El segundo tiempo
Shot	Un tiro
Sportswear	La ropa deportiva
Substitute	El suplente
Substitution	El cambio
Supporters, fans	La hinchada, los hinchas, los fanáticos
The post	El palo
The referee	El árbitro
To cheer	Animar
To play	Jugar
To score	Marcar
Yellow card	La tarjeta amarilla

PHRASES

English	Spanish
Goal!	¡Gol!

English	Spanish
Run!	¡Corre!
Do you want to play football?	¿Quieres jugar al fútbol?
Blow the whistle.	Sonar el silabato.
I play tennis.	Juego al tenis.
I'm not very sporty.	No soy muy deportista.
What a brilliant match!	¡Qué partidazo!
What is the score?	¿Cuál es el resultado?
What's your favorite team?	¿Cuál es tu deporte favorito?
I like to run three miles a day.	A mí me gusta correr tres millas diario.
Who won the game?	¿Quién ganó el juego?
Football is my favorite game.	El fútbol es mi juego favorite.
I like to play baseball.	Me gusta jugar el beisbol.
Which team is winning?	¿Cuál equipo está ganando el juego?
Give me the ball, please.	Dame la pelota, por favor.
It's your turn.	Te toca.
Would you like to go for a walk?	¿Te gustaría ir a caminar?

You can use the following YouTube videos for reference to enhance your accent and pronunciation:

- https://www.youtube.com/watch?v=NdNvXjIJz6s
    - [YouTube search: Spanish Vocabulary: Los Deportes – Sports]
- https://www.youtube.com/watch?v=h2-oRnBToBc
    - [YouTube search: Sports in Spanish : Deportes en Español]
- https://www.youtube.com/watch?v=tSErQSihsTM
    - [YouTube search: Sports in Spanish / Los Deportes]

If you're a sports fan, you'll find plenty of people to talk to in Spain, as it's a nation of sports fans.

CHAPTER EIGHTEEN

HOUSE AND FURNITURE

As we near the end of this book, let me give you some vocabulary for the various items you will probably have in the house.

Knowing all these will definitely make you feel more at home when speaking Spanish – pun intended!

English	Spanish
Apartment	El Apartamento
Closet	El Armario
Bucket	El Balde
Mailbox	El Buzón
Drawer	El Cajón
Lawn	El Césped
Cigarette	El Cigarrillo
Cigar	El Cigarro /El Puro
Cushion	El Cojín
Mattress	El Colchón
Dining Room	El Comedor
Freezer	El Congelador
Picture	El Cuadro
Compact Disc	El Disco Compacto
Desk	El Escritorio

English	Spanish
Mirror	El Espejo
Fire	El Fuego
Hook	El Gancho
Garage	El Garaje
Oven	El Horno
Microwave Oven	El Horno Microondas
Garden	El Jardín
CD Player	El Lector De CD
DVD Player	El Lector De DVD
Kerosene	El Petróleo
Clock	El Reloj
Corner	El Rincón
Floor	El Suelo
Ceiling	El Techo
Dresser	El Tocador
Cupboard	La Alacena

English	Spanish
Carpet	La Alfombra
Pillow	La Almohada
Light Bulb	La Bombilla
Camcorder	La Cámara
House	La Casa
Fence	La Cerca
Lock	La Cerradura
Hearth	La Chimenea
Cassette	La Cinta
Kitchen	La Cocina
Computer	La Computadora
Curtain	La Cortina
Pantry	La Despensa
Driveway	La Entrada Del Garaje
Ladder	La Escalera
Flower	La Flor
Lamp	La Lámpara

English	Spanish
Flashlight	La Linterna
Flame	La Llama
Key	La Llave
Camera	La Cámara
Film	La Película
Iron (Flat)	La Plancha
Floor (Levels)	La Planta /El Piso
Ground Floor	La Planta Baja
Door	La Puerta
Living Room	La Sala
Candle	La Vela
Front Walk	La Vereda
Matches	Las Cerillas
Storey/ floor	El Piso
Sideboard	El Aparador
Vacuum Cleaner	El Aspirador

English	Spanish
Poker	El Atizador
Balcony	El Balcón
Bathroom	El Baño
Ashtray	El Cenicero
Switch	El Conmutador / El Interruptor
Room	El Cuarto
Alarm Clock	El Despertador
Attic	El Desván
Record	El Disco
Bedroom	El Dormitorio / La Alcoba
Shelf	El Estante
Study	El Estudio
Sink	El Fregadero
Tap (Faucet)	El Grifo
Smoke	El Humo
Toilet (WC)	El Inodoro

Yard	El Jardín
Vase	El Jarrón
Sink (Bathroom)	El Lavabo
VCR	La Vídeo casetera
Wall (House)	El Muro
Refrigerator	El Refrigerador
Armchair	El Sillón
Sofa	El Sofá
Basement	El Sótano
Roof	El Tejado
Telephone	El Teléfono
Television	El Televisor
Pipe (Water)	El Tubo
Rug	La Alfombrilla
Bathtub	La Bañera
Box	La Caja

Bed	La Cama
Doorbell	La Campanilla
Basket	La Cesta
Chimney	La Chimenea
Blanket	La Cobija
Shower	La Ducha
Broom	La Escoba
Stove	La Estufa
Bookcase	La Librería
Table	La Mesa
Shovel	La Pala
Wall (Room)	La Pared
Blinds	La Persiana
Pipe	La Tubería
Radio	La Radio
Sheet	La Sábana
Sitting Room	La Sala

Chair	La Silla
Towel	La Toalla
Toaster	La Tostadora
Window	La Ventana
Stairs	Las Escaleras
Batteries	Las Pilas
Steps	Los Escalones
Furniture	Los Muebles

With everything you have learnt so far, I am confident that you can pronounce the different words above with great fluency without needing any YouTube video to confirm that what you are pronouncing is correct. Therefore, I won't provide any video tutorials in this section.

Before we close the book, it may be a good idea talk about a few mistakes that you may make innocently as you try to speak Spanish, so that you can take action to avoid them. While Spanish is a fairly straightforward language, there are a number of pitfalls for the unwary.

CHAPTER NINETEEN

COMMON MISTAKES MADE AS PEOPLE LEARN SPANISH

Beginners in Spanish make a lot of mistakes. You shouldn't be ashamed, since it happens to everybody. Consider it a stepping stone in your successful learning process. As you know, practice makes perfect – also, anyone who never made a mistake never made anything. It requires patience and practice for you to speak like a native Spanish speaker. Just speak and don't feel embarrassed when doing it. Make your learning fun by learning to learn from the mistakes you make. As you do this, you feel much more comfortable and confident as you speak Spanish, and this will boost your learning speed, as well as giving you and your Spanish friends something to laugh about.

The following are some of the mistakes many people make on their quest to learn Spanish, but if you pay attention to this section, then I highly doubt you will be making the same mistakes.

FALSE FRIENDS

As you learn Spanish, you may assume that the Spanish words that look almost the same as English words have the same meaning. Don't fall into this trap. Some words may have the same meaning, but others may have a very different meaning.

Below are a few examples.

Spanish	False friend	Actual Meaning
Soportar	Support	Tolerate
Once	Once	Eleven
Librería	Library	Bookshop
Importe	Import	Amount
Firma	Firm	Signature
Éxito	Exit	Success
Embarazada	Embarrassed	Pregnant
Cualidad	Quality	Characteristics
Carta	Card	Letter

Learning more of these words will help you avoid embarrassing situations as you speak. What is most important is to master how they are pronounced in context, just to make sure that you don't end up saying the wrong word with the same spelling.

SENTENCE ORDER

This is another common mistake you should be careful of. You may at times use the sentence order of your native language to translate your thoughts into Spanish sentences. Direct translation of individual words (literal translation) in a sentence is a common mistake for beginners learning all languages. It's what Google and other online translators often do (although not always), and it's incorrect. Avoid it at all costs. In particular, remember that, in Spanish, the noun always goes before the adjective, so *un vestido rojo* (literally _a dress red') is what you would say if you wanted to buy a red dress.

GENDER OF WORDS

This is yet another common mistake of almost all new language learners. Look out for words that may look feminine but are actually masculine, such as: *el día, el programa, el clima, el tema, el sistema, el mapa, el problema, el sofá, el planeta* and *el idioma*.

Another confusing gender trick is that words ending in _dad' are feminine. Usually, nouns ending in consonants are masculine. Think *la electricidad, la calidad, la universidad.*

To avoid making this mistake, make sure you get the gender (la or el) of a new word as you learn it. If you're not sure, check it in a dictionary – that will always tell you the correct gender

DATE

In English, the noun 'date' can either mean 'a day on the calendar' or 'a romantic or social appointment with someone/engagement'. This is not the same in Spanish: you use the words ―fecha‖ and ―cita‖ respectively when talking about the two.

MISUSE OF THE WORD "AMERICAN"

If you are a United States national, you are probably used to referring to yourself as an ―American.‖ In Spanish, an ―*Americano*‖ is a person from anywhere in South or North America. To say ―I am from the United States,‖ you should use the phrase, ―*Soy de los Estados Unidos*‖ so as to avoid any confusion.

CHAPTER TWENTY

SHORT STORIES AND QUESTIONS

Short stories are an integral part of the human experience. Culturally and historically, stories have allowed us to keep memories, experiences, myths, legends, accidents and incidents (among many other things) alive through time. Without stories, we would not be where we are today. For example, many children learn what to do and what not to do from stories told by their parents. Without these stories, a lot of us would not have the knowledge that we have today. Stories also allow us to bond with one another, communicating experiences of importance and reminiscing on past events that were significant in our lives. Stories make each and every one of us who we are, and all of us have thousands of stories that need to be told. Each language you speak is a different way to tell each story, and each culture and language tells stories differently than the next.

Pulling all the rules and words together to form sentences and a story that you can effectively communicate to another person is a huge accomplishment. Practicing these stories and questions will help you to improve your ability to transition from one sentence to the next. Short stories are great for improving your ability to explain and describe scenarios and happenings in your everyday life. Being able to tell stories is one of the first big steps in transitioning to conversation, which is arguably the hardest part of learning any new language.

Below are two short stories and questions for you to practice and go over.

Short Story Number One

Spanish

Manuel está de pie en línea en el aeropuerto. Él camina hasta el mostrador cuando es su turno. La recepcionista en el mostrador le pregunta por su ID y ella comprueba sus datos de bus. Sí, que se confirma en el vuelo 1103 de Dallas a Nueva York a las 3 pm.

Lleve sus bolsas para sentarse y esperar hasta que llegue el avión. El empleado imprime el billete y se lo da a él. Los agentes de seguridad a pie por él con un perro grande. El perro está olfateando alrededor de los bolsos de las personas que tratan de detectar drogas o explosivos. Manuel se alivia cuando el perro pasa por su lado. El perro se da vuelta y comienza a oler su bolsa y empieza a ladrar. El agente de seguridad mira a Manuel. —Señor, por favor, ven conmigo y llevar su bolsa.‖

Manuel pone a la defensiva inmediatamente. Él sabe que no tiene nada para que el perro ladrando se acerca. Se dice que los oficiales, —no tengo nada‖, pero el oficial de seguridad lo acompaña hasta el lado. —Vamos a ser el juez de eso‖ declaró el oficial de seguridad y comenzó a buscar. Su equipaje fue llevado y recogido a través, y luego la bolsa se empuja a través de otro escáner y luego recogió a través de nuevo. —Por favor, tome asiento por allí,‖ el oficial de seguridad señaló por encima de las sillas donde había otras personas esperar demasiado. Manuel se sentó rápidamente. Él no estaba contento el retraso causado este y con la esperanza de que no se pierda su avión. Manuel no le gusta llegar tarde.

English

Manuel is standing in line at the airport. He walks up to the counter when it is his turn. The clerk at the counter asks him for his ID and she checks his bus details. Yes, he is confirmed on flight 1103 from Dallas to New York at 3pm. He carries his bags to sit and wait until the plane arrives. The clerk prints out his ticket and hands it to him. The security officers walk by him with a large dog. The dog is sniffing around people's bags trying to detect drugs or explosives. Manuel is relieved when the dog walks past him. The dog turns and starts to sniff his bag and begins to bark. The security officer looks at Manuel. —Sir, please come with me and bring your bag.‖

Manuel becomes defensive immediately. He knows that he has nothing for the dog to be barking about. He says to the officers,

―I don't have anything,‖ but the security officer escorts him to the side. ―We will be the judge of that,‖ the security officer stated and began to search him. His luggage was taken and picked through, and then the bag was pushed through another scanner and then picked through again. ―Please take a seat over there,‖ the security officer pointed over to chairs where there were others waiting too. Manuel quickly sat down. He was not happy about the delay this caused and hoping that he doesn't miss his plane. Manuel doesn't like being late.

English Questions & Answers

(Please see the next section for a Spanish version of these questions and answers.)

Question 1: Where is Manuel waiting?

Answer 1: Manuel is waiting in line at the bus station.

Question 2: What is the abbreviation for ―identification‖?

Answer 2: The abbreviation for ―identification‖ is ID.

Question 3: What time is Manuel's flight scheduled to leave from Dallas?

Answer 3: His bus is scheduled to leave Dallas at 3 pm.

Question 4: In order to get on his plane, what document does Manuel have to have?

Answer 4: In order to get on the plane, Manuel will need his plane ticket.

Question 5: What are the security officers searching for with the sniffing dogs?

Answer 5: The dogs are sniffing and searching for explosives and drugs that may be hidden in people's bags.

Question 6: What is one thing that Manuel can't stand? Why does he believe he may be late or miss his bus?

Answer 6: Manuel can't stand to be late, and he is worried that this security check will cause him to either miss his bus or be late arriving to it, causing unnecessary stress. There is no indication of Manuel missing his bus, but he is worried about the potential for it to happen.

Spanish Questions & Answers

Pregunta 1: ¿Dónde está Manuel esperando?

Respuesta 1: Manuel está en el aeropuerto esperando en la cola.

Pregunta 2: ¿Cuál es la abreviatura de —identificación‖?

Respuesta 2: La abreviatura de "identificación" es ID.

Pregunta 3: ¿A qué hora es el vuelo de Manuel programado para salir de Dallas?

Respuesta 3: Su autobús está programado para salir de Dallas a las 3 pm.

Pregunta 4: Con el fin de conseguir en su avión, lo que hace Manuel documento tiene que tener?

Respuesta 4: Con el fin de subir al avión, Manuel necesitará su billete de avión.

Pregunta 5: ¿Cuáles son los agentes de seguridad en busca de los perros detectores?

Respuesta 5: Los perros olfatean y la búsqueda de explosivos y drogas que pueden estar ocultos en bolsas de las personas.

Pregunta 6: ¿Qué es una cosa que Manuel no puede soportar? ¿Por qué cree que puede llegar tarde o faltar su autobús?

Respuesta 6: Manuel no puede soportar estar tarde, y que está preocupado de que esta comprobación de seguridad le hará que sea menos su autobús o llegue tarde a la misma, causando un estrés innecesario. No hay ninguna indicación de Manuel extrañar a su autobús, pero que está preocupado por la posibilidad de que suceda.

Phrases for Practice

Listed below are some common statements and phrases that are often used by people who are traveling by plane. These phrases are first stated in English and then translated to Spanish; practicing them out loud can help you retain them more quickly.

English: You can get your boarding online.

Spanish: Usted puede obtener su tarjeta de embarque en línea .

English: We are traveling first class.

Spanish: Estamos viajando en primera clase .

English: Is is safe to travel by plane?

Spanish: Es es seguro viajar en avión?

English: I am not carrying any drugs in my luggage.

Spanish: No estoy llevando a alguna droga en mi equipaje .

English: We are traveling economy class.

Spanish: Estamos viajando en clase turista .

English: My mother is traveling first class.

Spanish: Mi madre está viajando en primera clase .

English: Do not panic, it is only a little wind and turbulence.

Spanish: No se asuste , es sólo un poco de viento y turbulencia .

English: When will we be taking off?

Spanish: ¿Cuándo vamos a estar empezando a despegar ?

English: We have already landed. Let's find our gate.

Spanish: Ya hemos aterrizado . Vamos a encontrar nuestra puerta .

English: The flight was rough but the flight attendant was calm.

Spanish: El vuelo era peligrosa, pero la azafata estaba en calma .

English: The pilot is making an announcement.

Spanish: El piloto está haciendo un anuncio .

English: We are flying in business class.

Spanish: Estamos volando en clase ejecutiva.

English: Hurry or we will miss our flight.

Spanish: Prisa o vamos a perder nuestro vuelo.

English: Does this seat lay back?

Spanish: ¿Este asiento se echó hacia atrás ?

English: Drinks and Snacks will be served.

Spanish: Se servirán bebidas y aperitivos .

English: What time will we arrive?

Spanish: ¿A qué hora vamos a llegar?

English: Sir, would you like a drink?

Spanish: Señor, ¿quieres un trago?

English: This is a connecting flight. I have to change flights at California.

Spanish: Se trata de un vuelo de conexión . Tengo que cambiar los vuelos en California.

English: I will have to call the airline to confirm.

Spanish: Voy a tener que llamar a la compañía aérea para confirmar .

English: The pilot had to make an emergency landing.

Spanish: El piloto tuvo que realizar un aterrizaje de emergencia.

English: The landing was smooth, but the flight was a little rough.

Spanish: El aterrizaje fue suave, pero el vuelo era un poco peligroso.

English: I don't like flying, it makes me nervous.

Spanish: No me gusta volar, me pone nervioso.

English: My luggage won't fit in the overhead compartment.

Spanish: Mi equipaje no cabe en el compartimiento superior.

English: I have to check this suitcase. I will take the smaller one as a carry-on.

Spanish: Tengo que revisar esta maleta. Voy a tomar la más pequeña como equipaje de mano.

English: I need one day to get over the jet lag.

Spanish: Necesito un día para superar el jet lag.

English: We will be landing soon.

Spanish: Aterrizaremos pronto.

English: We are late for our flight.

Spanish: Llegamos tarde para nuestro vuelo.

SHORT STORY NUMBER TWO

Spanish

Michael y su amigo Mark están explorando un nuevo país en un coche que han alquilado. Su próxima aventura es encontrar un restaurante con el nombre de —La mejor hamburguesa en la ciudad‖, debido a las críticas positivas que se han hecho que señalan que el restaurante no tiene —la mejor hamburguesa en la ciudad.‖ Sin embargo, ahora se encuentran perdidos. Se les dio instrucciones que eran imposibles de seguir y que han estado conduciendo durante horas. Ellos encuentran un extraño caminando por la carretera y que parece ser local en la zona y es posible que puedan ayudarles a descubrir qué dirección deben ir en. Se detienen y le piden dirección. El desconocido sonríe y responde: —Oh, ese es mi lugar favorito. Es fácil de llegar y yo le puede decir cómo.‖ Mark agarra un lápiz y papel para tomar notas acerca y escucha como el extraño se les da direcciones.

—Siga recto hasta que vea un granero con una puerta rota.

Gire a la derecha después de que el granero y continuar en pasar dos árboles grandes en el lado derecho. Cuando se llega a un arbusto a una milla, que se parece a una araña gigante, de miedo pero cierto., Gire a la derecha en ese arbusto y seguir recto durante otros quince minutos. Usted debe pasar una gasolinera a la derecha. Unos diez minutos después de la gasolinera, verá tres pilas de arena y una casa con una vaca atada a un árbol. A la derecha en la casa y el restaurante que busca será el segundo restaurante a su izquierda. La luz de la muestra están rotos y que es un poco difícil de leer, pero no se puede perder. Cuenta con una roca al lado de él que se parece a un mono con un cuchillo. Algunas personas estarán fuera bailando y bebiendo cerveza.

Buena suerte y buen viaje! Marcos levantó la vista de sus notas que había escrito las instrucciones sobre. —¿Recibió todo eso?, Preguntó Micheal Marcos. quien los recita de nuevo para confirmar que los había conseguido derecha. Marcos se rió para sí mismo mientras leía sobre las direcciones de nuevo, —esto debe ser divertido, dijo a sí mismo. Se ponen de nuevo en el coche y comienzan en la carretera siguiendo las instrucciones proporcionadas. Antes de darse cuenta, que son la identificación de los puntos de referencia que el desconocido les dijo que iban a ver y están haciendo su camino rápidamente hacia el restaurante.

Después de ver la roca que parece que podría ser un mono con un cuchillo, los hombres se fijan en el signo estallado frente del restaurante.

Marcos levantó la vista de su bloc de notas que había escrito las instrucciones sobre. —¿Recibió todo eso?‖, Preguntó Micheal Marcos. Quien los recita de nuevo para confirmar que los había conseguido derecha. Marcos se rió para sí mismo mientras leía sobre las direcciones de nuevo, —esto debe ser divertido‖, dijo a sí mismo . Se ponen de nuevo en el coche y comienzan en la carretera siguiendo las instrucciones proporcionadas . Antes de darse cuenta , que son la identificación de los puntos de referencia que el desconocido les dijo que iban a ver y están haciendo su camino rápidamente hacia el restaurante . Después de ver la roca que parece que podría ser un mono con un cuchillo , los hombres se fijan en el signo estallado frente del restaurante.

English

Micheal and his friend Mark are exploring a new country in a car they have rented. Their next adventure is to find a restaurant by the name of —The Best Hamburger in Town‖ because of the positive reviews that have been made that said the restaurant does have —The Best Hamburger in Town.‖ But , they are now find themselves lost. They were given directions that were impossible to follow and they have been driving around for hours. They find a stranger walking down the road and he seems to be local to the area and it is possible he can help them find out which direction they should be going in. They stop and ask him for direction. The stranger smiles and replies: ―Oh, that's my favorite place. It is simple to get there and I can tell you how.‖ Mark grabs a pen and paper to take notes on and listens as the stranger gives them directions.

―Go straight until you see a barn with a broken gate. Make a right after that barn and continue on until you pass two large trees on the right-hand side. When you come to a bush about a mile down, that looks like a giant spider, scary but true. Turn right at that bush and keep going straight for another fifteen minutes. You should pass a gas station on your right. About ten minutes after the gas station, you will see three piles of sand and a house with a cow tied to a tree. Make a right at that house and the restaurant you are looking for will be the second restaurant on your left. The sign light are broken and it is a bit difficult to read, but you can't miss it. It has a rock next to it that looks like a monkey holding a knife. Some people will be outside dancing and drinking. Good luck and safe travels!"

Mark looked up from his notepad that he had written the directions on. ―Did you get all that?‖ Micheal asked Mark. He recited them back to confirm he had got them right. Mark giggled to himself as he read over the directions again, —This should be fun,‖ he said to himself. They get back into the car and begin down the road following the directions provided. Before they know it, they are identifying the landmarks that the stranger told them they would see and are making their way quickly towards the restaurant. After seeing the rock that looks as though it could be a monkey holding a knife, the men notice the broken sign out front of the restaurant.

—This must be it! We found it!‖ Micheal cheered, doubtful of the direction's accuracy to begin with. —Who would have thought we could find a place based on a handful of strange landmarks,‖ Mark stated, crumbling up the note with the written directions and threw it into the floorboard of the vehicle. A gust of wind blew the receipt back out of the floor of the car and onto the dusty driveway of the restaurant. As the men walked inside the restaurant by the name of —The Best Hamburger In Town‖ the crumpled-up directions bounced down the road like a tumbleweed in the desert.

English Questions & Answers

(Please see the next section for a Spanish version of these questions and answers.)

Question One: What is the name of the restaurant that Mark and Michael are looking for?

Answer One: The name of the restaurant that Mark and Michael are looking for is called, ―The Best Hamburger In Town.‖

Question Two: Why are Mark and Michael lost?

Answer Two: Mark and Michael are lost because they are in an unfamiliar country, and the directions they were given were nearly impossible to understand.

Question Three: What do Mark and Michael do to get directions to the restaurant they are looking for?

Answer Three: The men pull over and talk to a stranger who is local to the area and knows how to get to ―The Best Hamburger in Town.‖

Question Four: Are the directions that were provided by the stranger easy to follow?

Answer Four: They are complicated and based on landmarks so, for people who are from the city, it may be a bit difficult to understand or follow.

Question Five: Why can't they read the sign out in front of the restaurant?

Answer Five: The sign is broken and difficult to read. Instead of the sign, they are looking for a rock next to the restaurant that has the appearance of the bear holding a sword.

Question Six: Were Michael and Mark able to find the restaurant using the landmarks provided by the stranger on the side of the road?

Answer Six: Yes, Michael and Mark found the restaurant using the directions and landmarks provided by the stranger on the side of the road. Both men were surprised at the accuracy of the directions and were surprised when they arrived at their destination.

Spanish Questions & Answers

Primera pregunta: ¿Cuál es el nombre del restaurante que Mark y Michael están buscando?

Una Respuesta: El nombre del restaurante que Mark y Michael están buscando se llama, ―La mejor hamburguesa en la ciudad.‖

Segunda pregunta: ¿Por qué son Mark y Michael perdieron?

Respuesta dos: Mark y Michael se pierden debido a que no están en un país familiar y se les dio instrucciones que eran casi imposibles de seguir.

Tercera pregunta: ¿Cómo Mark y Michael reciben las instrucciones para el restaurante que está buscando?

Respuesta Tres: Los hombres tiran una y piden un extraño desconocido que es de la zona y dice que sabe cómo llegar a "La mejor hamburguesa en la ciudad."

Cuarta pregunta: ¿Son las instrucciones que se proporcionaron por el local de fácil de seguir?

Cuatro responder: Son difíciles de entender y sólo sobre la base de puntos de referencia por lo que, para las personas que son de la ciudad, puede ser un poco difícil de comprender o seguir.

Cinco pregunta: ¿Qué está mal con el signo en frente del restaurante?

Responde a cinco: La muestra se rompe y difícil de leer. Se les dice a buscar una roca al lado del restaurante que se ve como un mono con un cuchillo.

Seis pregunta: ¿Fueron Michael y Mark capaz de encontrar el restaurante usando los puntos de referencia proporcionados por el desconocido en el lado de la carretera?

Respuesta Seis: Sí, Michael y Mark encontraron el restaurante con las direcciones y puntos de referencia que el desconocido en el lado de la carretera proporcionada. Los dos hombres fueron sorprendidos por la claridad de las instrucciones y se mostraron complacidos cuando lograron hasta el restaurante.

Phrases for Practice

Listed below are some common statements and phrases that are often used by people who are traveling via automobile. These phrases are first stated in English and then translated to Spanish; practicing them out loud can help you retain them more quickly.

English: How do I get to the highway from here?

Spanish: ¿Cómo llego a la carretera desde aquí?

English: Go south for 15 kilometers and make a right.

Spanish: Vaya hacia el sur durante 15 kilómetros y gire a la derecha .

English: U-turns are illegal, you can't do those here.

Spanish: Las vueltas en U son ilegales , no se puede hacer esos artículos aquí.

English: Roads don't have pavement, it will damage my tires.

Spanish: Las carreteras no tienen pavimento , se puede dañar los neumáticos .

English: Make a left at the gas station. You will see the fire station on the left.

Spanish: Gire a la izquierda en la gasolinera . Verá la estación de bomberos de la izquierda .

English: This is a one-way street.

Spanish: Esta es una calle de un sólo sentido.

English: Police are directing traffic since the traffic lights aren't working.

Spanish: La policía está dirigiendo el tráfico desde los semáforos no están funcionando .

English: This address isn't on the map, how do I find it?

Spanish: Esta dirección no está en el mapa , ¿cómo lo encuentro?

English: We are lost, do you know where we are?

Spanish: Estamos perdidos , sabes dónde estamos?

English: I took the wrong exit on the highway. I am completely lost.

Spanish: Tomé la salida equivocada en la carretera. Estoy completamente perdido .

English: Her house is the one with the white picket fence in front.

Spanish: Su casa es el que tiene la valla blanca en la frente .

English: We didn't get lost! We just took the scenic route.

Spanish: Nosotros no perderse ! Tomamos la ruta escénica .

English: I think we made too many left turns. We passed this street an hour ago.

Spanish: Creo que hicimos demasiadas vueltas a la izquierda . Pasamos por esta calle una hora hace .

English: These directions are too difficult.

Spanish: Estas direcciones son demasiado difíciles .

English: The library is the second building on the left.

Spanish: La biblioteca es el segundo edificio a la izquierda .

English: The museum is behind the restaurant.

Spanish: El museo está detrás del restaurante .

English: The bookstore is in front of the museum.

Spanish: La librería está en frente del museo .

English: You need to enter in the back of the building.

Spanish: Es necesario introducir en la parte trasera del edificio .

English: There are no road signs here. You have to ask people for directions.

Spanish: No hay señales de tráfico aquí . Usted tiene que pedir a la gente por el camino.

English: How does Santa Claus find our homes? Does he have a really big map or does he use GPS now?

Spanish: ¿Cómo Santa Claus a encontrar en nuestras casas ? ¿Tiene un mapa muy grande o qué usa el GPS ahora?

English: Green means "Go," yellow means "slow", and red means "stop."

Spanish: El verde significa "Ve , " amarillo significa " lento" , y " parada ". Rojo

Significa.

English: Look both ways before turning right on red and yield to pedestrians.

Spanish: Mirar a ambos lados antes de girar a la derecha en rojo y ceder el paso a los peatones.

English: You cannot pass here.

Spanish: No se puede pasar aquí.

English: There is construction on this road so watch out for construction workers.

Spanish: Hay obras en esta carretera así que ten cuidado para trabajadores de la

construcción.

English: We took a wrong turn.

Spanish: Tomamos un camino equivocado.

English: We are lost.

Spanish: Estamos perdidos.

English: You are going over the speed limit.

Spanish: Que se va por encima del límite de velocidad.

English: You are going below the speed limit.

Spanish: Usted va por debajo del límite de velocidad.

English: Can you help me find this road?

Spanish: ¿Puede usted ayudarme a encontrar este camino ?

English: Can you help me find the nearest hospital?

Spanish: ¿Puede usted ayudarme a encontrar el hospital más cercano ?

English: Can you help me find the nearest gas station?

Spanish: ¿Puede usted ayudarme a encontrar la gasolinera más cercana ?

English: Can you help me find the nearest hotel?

Spanish: ¿Puede usted ayudarme a encontrar el hotel más cercano?

You can see that in the first short story, Manuel was traveling on an airline, which would require him to use a variety of different terms and phrases pertaining to traveling by air. The phrases and questions chosen were meant to provide you with different phrases you could use if you were traveling to a Spanish speaking country, easing some of your concerns about your ability to communicate with airline personnel and employees. In the second short story, Michael and Mark were lost while driving around in a new country, which can be highly stressful for people who aren't fluent in the country's dominant language. The second short story questions and phrases give you a variety of options if you are traveling and get lost on the road. There are also different expressions regarding the rules of the road and various phrases about traveling via automobile. With these short stories, we hope that you have learned a little more about conversational Spanish and how it can be used to help you in different ways.

CONCLUSION

As you have hopefully discovered, speaking Spanish is not difficult, especially when you have so many words to use in your everyday conversations. The best way to master the language is to hear Spanish speakers speak it, and converse with them. Anyone can learn from a book, but the best way to retain the language is to use it in everyday conversation. Getting to know the way in which certain words are used and learning how different people say different words can be difficult. This is because people who are fluent or native to a language may be lax on certain pronunciations and proper verbiage because they have adopted a more slang or relaxed language by nature. This is perfectly normal – you do it currently in the language you speak without even realizing it. This is why speaking to people conversationally is incredibly important in learning and retaining a new language.

You now should have all the information you need to speak and practice Spanish every day. Make use of that information by making friends with Spanish speakers, either in real life or online, and using what you have learned. Spanish is a fun language, and it's very colorful and expressive. Have fun with it, and have fun with the people who speak it as their native language!

KEY TAKEAWAYS

- The best way to learn Spanish or any other language is to collect as many phrases as possible, then look for videos that show how to pronounce them.

- When you have the phrases, you need to practice and listen to native speakers saying them.

- Don't rely on online translators like Google Translator to teach you the right accent or pronunciation.

- If you're a Little hesitant about practicing your Spanish because people speak too fast for you to pick up all the words, try reading Spanish newspapers to increase your vocabulary and give you more confidence. You'll be surprised how much you can understand!

- Learn as the children do – associate words with pictures. Pick up the special offer leaflets from the local stores each week and expand your vocabulary.

- The best way to master the accent is to listen to the different audio, speak to Spanish speakers and watch training videos where native speakers teach the language.

- You can learn a lot more when you have a passion for mastering Spanish.

- You really don't need to be a master of grammar to speak Spanish or any other language; in any case, most natives never learn the grammar themselves!

HOW TO PUT THIS INFORMATION INTO ACTION

1. Go to each chapter, try pronouncing the different words in that chapter, and then look for relevant YouTube videos to confirm your pronunciation. Practice as much as possible to master the pronunciation.
2. Go to the phrases section in each chapter and try pronouncing the words/phrases.
3. Go to YouTube or any other place you can search for relevant videos that will help you with the pronunciation.
4. Once you have mastered how to pronounce the words, go back to each chapter and try to pronounce them without referring to the videos.
5. Don't just stop at these phrases. Instead, you should seek to expand your knowledge of Spanish.
6. Have a friend or family member ask you the questions in the book and require you to answer them correctly. This will build your conversational skills which are some of the most important skills when learning a new language.
7. Do you know someone who speaks Spanish? Ask them to take the time, even if it's an hour on the phone occasionally and speak with you in conversation using the Spanish language.

This will give you the feel and practice of having an everyday conversation in Spanish.

BONUS RESOURCES

- Duolingo: https://www.duolingo.com/
- Foreign Services Institute: http://fsi-languagecourses.org/Content.php
- Omniglot Intro to Languages: http://www.omniglot.com/writing/languages.htm ☐ BBC Languages: http://www.bbc.co.uk/languages/other/quickfix/
- About's Language Specific Posts: http://www.about.com/education/ ☐ My Language Exchange: http://www.mylanguageexchange.com/
- Interpals: http://www.interpals.net/
- The Polygot Club: http://polyglotclub.com/
- Forvo: http://forvo.com/
- RhinoSpike: https://rhinospike.com/
- Google Translate: https://translate.google.com/
- Lang 8: http://lang-8.com/

www.ingramcontent.com/pod-product-compliance
Lightning Source LLC
Chambersburg PA
CBHW071413070526
44578CB00003B/563